CW00926315

Who Is the
HOLY SPIRIT?

Praise for *Who is the Holy Spirit?*

"Amos Yong has written a wonderful meditation on the Holy Spirit that explores who God's Spirit is, as well as how the Spirit's work penetrates every element of human existence. Fully conversant with contemporary approaches to biblical interpretation, Yong facilitates an illuminating conversation between Luke's Gospel and Acts to fashion a sacred space in which the reader can grow in understanding the Holy Spirit's practical importance in forming Christ's disciples for today's world. This book should be used in the local church or college classroom to initiate Christians into a richer, more profound appreciation of the empowering presence of the Third Person of the Holy Trinity."
—DR. ROBERT W. WALL, the Paul T. Walls Professor of Scripture and Wesleyan Studies, Seattle Pacific University

"Amos Yong's Who Is the Holy Spirit? *offers a fresh perspective on Luke-Acts. Although some before him have read together Jesus' story in Luke with the missions story of Acts, Yong provides new insights. By asking new questions traditionally neglected in approaches to Luke-Acts, he provides us new perspectives. As a biblical scholar, I have found these insights challenging and useful."*
—CRAIG S. KEENER, Professor of New Testament, Palmer Theological Seminary

"I strongly recommend this book on the Holy Spirit to individuals and communities seeking to be transformed so that they can do the Spirit's work when and where the Spirit may bring them about. Drawing on Acts and Luke to illuminate our own lives, it provides a rich resource for understanding how we might discern and participate in the Holy Spirit's work in our world today."
—LOIS MALCOLM, Associate Professor of Systematic Theology, Luther Seminary and Review Editor for the *Journal of the Society of Christian Ethics*

"How relevant is the Holy Spirit in today's world? Very, as Amos Yong makes clear in Who Is the Holy Spirit? *In a comprehensive approach that is both eminently readable and well-researched, Dr. Yong traces the work of the Holy Spirit in Luke-Acts through its myriad contemporary implications. A must-read for Christians!"*
—JANICE MCGRANE, SSJ, author of *Saints to Lean On: Spiritual Companions for Illness & Disability*

a PARACLETE GUIDE

Who Is the HOLY SPIRIT?

A WALK WITH THE APOSTLES

Amos Yong

PARACLETE PRESS
BREWSTER, MASSACHUSETTS

Who Is the Holy Spirit? A Walk with the Apostles

Copyright © 2011 by Amos Yong

ISBN 978-1-55725-635-5

Scripture references are taken from the New Revised Standard Version Bible, copyright © 1989 by the Division of Education of the National Council of Churches of Christ in the U.S.A., and are used by permission. All rights reserved.

Library of Congress Cataloging-in-Publication Data
Yong, Amos.
  Who is the Holy Spirit? : a walk with the Apostles / Amos Yong.
      p. cm.—(A Paraclete guide)
  Includes bibliographical references (p. 217) and index.
  ISBN 978-1-55725-635-5
  1. Holy Spirit—Biblical teaching. 2. Bible. N.T. Acts—Commentaries. 3.
Bible. N.T. Luke—Criticism, interpretation, etc. I. Title.
  BS2589.6.H62Y66 2011
  231'.3—dc22

                                    2011010838

10 9 8 7 6 5 4 3 2 1

All rights reserved. No portion of this book may be reproduced, stored in an electronic retrieval system, or transmitted in any form or by any means—electronic, mechanical, photocopy, recording, or any other—except for brief quotations in printed reviews, without the prior permission of the publisher.

Published by Paraclete Press
Brewster, Massachusetts
www.paracletepress.com
Printed in the United States of America

o Alyssa

With all my love.

Contents

INTRODUCTION

How Wide Is the World and Work
of the Holy Spirit?

I GREW UP in a Pentecostal-evangelical environment.
My life growing up was marked by a keen awareness
of the person and work of the Holy Spirit. I had a
series of ecstatic experiences of the Holy Spirit at
summer church camps during my teenage years, which left a deep
impression on my religious life. The gifts of the Holy Spirit that
were frequently manifested in our churches—speaking in tongues,
words of prophecy, healings—have shaped my understanding. I
am grateful to God for blessing me with the Pentecostalism of my
youth.

However, I've also come to see that, as valuable as these
experiences have been, they are only the tip of the iceberg, so to
speak, of the work of the Holy Spirit in the world. And by this, I
don't mean only that the Spirit has touched lives all over the world
like he has touched my own. I've also come to recognize that my
own view of the Spirit's person and work is too individualistic, too
spiritualistic, and too ecclesiocentric. In my pietistic upbringing,
for example, the work of the Spirit had to do with me: my salvation,
my sanctification, my experience of the Spirit's power touching
the lives of others in my church. I am not denying that these are
all important ways in which God meets human lives. However, I
concluded from this that the be-all and end-all of the Spirit's work
was to transform individuals.

Related to this was the sense that the work of the Holy Spirit was designed to purify me from this world and to prepare me spiritually for the life to come. Life in this world was important only as a testing and training ground, and the Spirit was the divine helper sent to prepare us for eternal life. Here, I was a pilgrim alongside other pilgrims, and together we were the body and church of Jesus Christ, cleansed and empowered by his Holy Spirit to bear witness to the world about the coming rule of God. So I thought the work of the Spirit was pretty much restricted to the Christian life and the life of the church.

Of course, the Spirit was also at work "out there" in the world, but only to convict unbelievers of their sin and to turn them to Christ. Here again, in the faith of my childhood the Spirit worked only at the level of the individual, focused primarily if not only on the spiritual dimension of individual lives, in order to transform and save them in light of the coming judgment of God and the world. I don't deny today that the Spirit remains active in the world in all of these ways, but I now believe there is so much more the Spirit is doing in the world beyond what I'd been trained to recognize. I now believe that the Spirit is at work not just at the level of the individual but also at the level of society and its various political and economic structures; not just at the otherworldly, spiritual level but also at the this-worldly level of the material and concrete domains of our lives; not just in and through the church but also in and through wider institutional, cultural, and even religious realities. In other words, I now think that the world of the Holy Spirit is much wider than I'd guessed, and that the work of the Spirit is to redeem and transform our world as a whole along with all of its interconnected parts, systems, and structures.

This book attempts to sketch such a vision of the person and work of the Holy Spirit by a careful rereading of the New Testament—particularly Luke-Acts. The author of this two-part work, known in the Christian tradition as Luke the physician, is not only the most prolific contributor to the New Testament but also the one who mentions the Holy Spirit more than any other. In fact, both the third Gospel and the Acts of the Apostles are often deemed as narratives about the works of the Holy Spirit.

Acts 1:8 says, "But you will receive power when the Holy Spirit has come upon you; and you will be my witnesses in Jerusalem, in all Judea and Samaria, and to the ends of the earth." The "you" refers to the disciples, who will testify of Jesus to the ends of the earth. Pause just a moment. Take note with me that there is a geographical progression going on here. Starting from Jerusalem (Acts 1:12–6:7), expanding outward from there through Judea and Samaria (6:8–9:31), and culminating in Rome (9:32–28:31)—the "ends of the earth" from the Jewish perspective centered in Jerusalem—this is precisely the outline of the book of Acts. So Acts tells us that the entire apostolic witness to the ends of the earth is empowered by the Holy Spirit.

In the chapters to follow we will see that the work of the Holy Spirit concerns both that of individual lives and the wider world, both the spiritual and the more mundane aspects of our existence, both the church and the wider public square. It will take us the rest of the book to fully understand this. Preliminarily, note that the events recorded in Luke-Acts occur within the realm of the Roman Empire. Hence there is an inevitable political dimension to the text; sometimes this is evident, other times it is "behind the text" or between the lines. I propose that if we read Luke-Acts as set within the matrix and under the shadow of imperial Rome, we will

see how the Holy Spirit's working in the lives of the earliest followers of Jesus is connected to the Spirit's activity in the politics of this
world. This may also help us link the work of Spirit in our personal
lives to that in national and international politics today.

There are also extensive passages throughout Luke-Acts that
address the social and economic dimension of human lives. These
themes are intertwined with the messianic mission of Jesus to
restore the kingdom to Israel. Yet such restoration involved neither a revolutionary form of nationalism hostile to the Gentiles (as
many first-century Jewish zealots had hoped for) nor a merely spiritual realization of "Israel" in the church (as previous supersessionist
theologies have posited). Instead, the restoration of Israel involved
a renewal and fulfillment of the ancient promise to Abraham—
that through his descendents, "all the families of the earth shall
be blessed" (Acts 3:25; cf. Gen. 12:3)—that simultaneously invited
the participation of all the peoples of the earth in the messianic
kingdom of peace, justice, and righteousness. I believe that the two
books of Luke and Acts will also illuminate what the Spirit is doing
in our social arrangements and in our economies, even the global
economy today.

Finally, as already noted, the apostolic horizons are global:
"to the ends of the earth." This concern about the whole world
includes the diversity of languages, the broad spectrum of people
groups (Jews and Gentiles, men and women, young and old, slave
and free), and all cultures and ethnicities. In that sense, I believe
that this study can help us understand what the Spirit might be
doing today in a world of multiculturalism, class stratification,
diversity, and pluralism.

Above all, if we can see how the Holy Spirit empowered Jesus
and his followers to announce in their words and enact in their

deeds the arrival of the coming kingdom of God, this might help us to discern and participate in the work of the Holy Spirit in the world today. The following quest reflects my desire to discern the Spirit's work in our world, not only so that we can be better witnesses to those "outside," but also that we may be transformed as individual followers of Jesus and as members of a community of believers seeking to do the works of Christ whenever and wherever the Spirit may bring them about.[1]

Our study will proceed as follows. We will begin with the book of Acts and pretty much follow the narrative sequentially as laid out by Luke. This will help us to enter into the world of the earliest followers of Jesus the Messiah, to follow their footsteps as they were empowered by the Holy Spirit. By so doing, we will see the Holy Spirit at work in individual lives, empowering them to proclaim and live out the messiahship and lordship of Jesus Christ in the world. But because the earliest believers lived out of their memory of Jesus, in almost every other chapter, we will glance "back," historically speaking, from Acts to the Gospel of Luke itself, in order to glimpse just how the followers of Jesus might have been inspired by his Spirit-filled life, ministry, and teachings as they negotiated their own challenges of being in but not of the world. Proceeding in this way does what I had been raised to do: reread our present life in light of the lives of the apostles so as to allow their experiences to illuminate our own.

As I will be staying pretty close to the text of Acts and Luke, given our approach, I strongly recommend keeping a copy of the New Testament closely at hand. We will observe how the central role played by the kingdom of God in the Spirit-empowered lives of Jesus and his followers enriches our quest to discern the work of the Holy Spirit in our lives today. But ours is an interpretive approach that has by and large been absent in most devotional, homiletic, and commentary interactions with the Lukan writings. My intention will be to spend most of our time in each chapter exploring how the work of the Spirit to bring about the kingdom has wider implications for understanding the message and demands of the gospel.

The eight parts of this book follow the path of the apostles as recorded in the book of Acts as intimated in 1:8—"But you will receive power when the Holy Spirit has come upon you; and you will be my witnesses in Jerusalem, in all Judea and Samaria, and to the ends of the earth." Breaking up the many chapters of the book into these more manageable parts will help us walk with the apostles and learn with them as their own horizons were continuously expanded in following the work of the Holy Spirit from Jerusalem through Judea and Samaria to the ends of the earth. This will in turn give rise to questions about how to see the work of the Holy Spirit in our lives, in our churches, and in our world today. My goal in these studies, however, is to be less prescriptive about how to respond to these contemporary questions than to open up some biblical and theological "space" for these questions to emerge, and for present-day followers of Jesus to discuss and explore the issues. Hence the discussion questions at the end of the book are correlated with each chapter and meant to stimulate church, college, or study group conversation about the work of the Spirit in the world. I am convinced that if we pay careful attention to how the Holy Spirit worked through Jesus and his followers to transform their world, so also will we be in a better place to listen to the voice of the Holy Spirit as he speaks to and leads us today in that same task.

PART ONE

The Outpouring of the Holy Spirit

1

The Acts of the Holy Spirit and the Kingdom of God

Acts 1; Luke 22:24-30

N THE FIRST BOOK, Theophilus, I wrote about all that Jesus did and taught from the beginning," is what Acts 1:1 says. Luke is referring of course to the Gospel of Luke as that "first book." It too was dedicated to Theophilus. The original readers of these volumes, Theophilus and those in his community, were either citizens or, more probably, residents of the Roman Empire. It's amid this reality that we are being introduced to the teachings about and the inauguration of the kingdom of God.

Jesus taught his disciples about the kingdom during the forty days between his resurrection and ascension (Acts 1:3). Jesus' teachings about the kingdom during this period were at least in part about his own life and ministry, as foretold by the Scriptures (Lk. 24:44–46). But his life was intimately linked to the kingdom, in terms of both what he proclaimed and what he did. In other words, in the life and teachings of Jesus, the kingdom of God comes up against and even confronts the kingdoms of this world, the latter being most prominently represented by King Herod of Judea (1:5) and Emperors Augustus (2:1) and Tiberius (3:1) of the Roman Empire.

In Jesus' last exchange with the disciples before his ascension, their urgent question to him was, "Lord, is this the time when you will restore the kingdom to Israel?" (Acts 1:6). This question reflects the assumption that (minimally) the Messiah would overthrow the Roman rule immediately, enable Israel to repossess the land promised to their ancestors, and usher in Yahweh's reign over Zion. But more than this, the question also reflected the disciples' own self-understanding about the specific role they would play in the new kingdom of Israel. After all, Jesus had appointed the Twelve as leaders of the new Israel and promised that they would "eat and drink at my table in my kingdom, and . . . will sit on thrones judging the twelve tribes of Israel" (Lk. 22:30).

But part of the problem was that one of the Twelve (Judas) had defected and was no longer among them. Understanding their situation in light of scriptural resources (Acts 1:16–20; cf. Ps. 69:25; 109:8), the remaining eleven were led to cast lots for two nominated brothers, who met strict criteria, in order to prepare for their reign in the coming kingdom. Yet the "elected" individual, Matthias, never gets mentioned again in the Acts of the Apostles. This entire episode reveals that the disciples did not anticipate the renewal of Israel would take a very different shape.

In response to their question about when the kingdom would appear, Jesus said: "It is not for you to know the times or periods that the Father has set by his own authority. But you will receive power when the Holy Spirit has come upon you; and you will be my witnesses in Jerusalem, in all Judea and Samaria, and to the ends of the earth" (Acts 1:7–8). In one sense, Jesus' answer to their question is no: the times and periods of the restoration of the kingdom of Israel remain unknown, resting only in the authority of the Father. Yet during this interim period the apostles will be given the power of the Holy Spirit in order to bear witness to the life and ministry of the one who proclaimed and did the works of the kingdom. So, even if the direct response to the disciples' question is negative, the indirect response is more complicated: while we may not know when the full restoration of Israel will happen, we will nevertheless be empowered to proclaim the teachings and do the deeds of the Messiah himself. In this case, the actual answer to the disciples' question depends on the extent to which they are open to receiving the kingdom and living it out through the Spirit's power.

The gift of the Holy Spirit empowers the disciples' witnesses to the ends of the earth. This is no generic witness, but one that is specific to geographic regions like Jerusalem, Judea, Samaria, and even to the heart of the empire, Rome itself. In other words, not only does the Spirit empower the disciples' witness to the kingdom teachings and realities of Jesus, but the Spirit does so in order to establish the kingdom amid the present imperial rule of Caesar and his regional governments. So when the disciples then go forth to proclaim the kingdom, they do so with the full reality of the Roman Empire pressing down on them.

No doubt there were various views among the earliest followers of Jesus regarding the relationship between the kingdom of God and the empire of Rome. Some discounted any link, saying that the divine kingdom has to do with the next world and hence has no relation to the Roman Empire. Others believed that the empire was more friendly than not to Christian interests, and perhaps Luke wrote in part to convince Roman leaders that Christians were not troublemakers (rather, Jews were), or even that Christians were actually model citizens who deserved all of the political benefits given to religious practitioners throughout the empire. And there was probably also a third group that believed Jesus' teachings and deeds challenged the social, economic, and political structures of imperial Rome.

The Acts of the Apostles are also the acts of the Holy Spirit in the church, acts that are subversive of the empires of this world. The story of the early church should be understood as the establishment and emergence of a community that proclaimed and embodied the messianic life and teachings of Jesus against the cultic, political, and economic structures of the Roman Empire in the first century. How then should contemporary readers of Luke-Acts live amid the powers of this world, wherever they might be—whether that of China in the Far East, of the Organization of the Islamic Conference, of the European Union, of America, or even of the empire of global market consumerism? While it will take us the rest of this book to answer these questions concretely, let me say for the moment that the key to our response lies precisely in Jesus' response to the disciples' question about when the kingdom would be restored to Israel: in the gift of the Holy Spirit. The empowering witness of the Spirit has been and will continue to be central to how Christians live faithfully in a world of many oftentimes conflicting powers. Whether the demands on our lives are imposed by governments, social systems, or the global economy, it is the Holy Spirit who enables the proper and appropriate response that is sensitive to the variables of each situation. The Spirit who effectively empowered the acts of the apostles during the *Pax Romana* is the same Spirit who is available to followers of the Messiah today.

2

Promising to Restore the Kingdom of Israel, and the Spirit Came!

Luke 1:46-55, 67-79; 2:22-38

UT WHAT EXACTLY WERE THE DISCIPLES EXPECTING with regard to Jesus and the kingdom of God? We've already seen that the Jewish hopes regarding the kingdom were connected to the Messiah, who would free them from foreign rule. More precisely, the coming of the kingdom would restore the land of Israel according to the covenants made with Abraham, Moses, and David. Now let's focus our attention on what the disciples as well as Luke's readers had been led to expect regarding what the Messiah would accomplish. To do so, we should look carefully at a number of passages from the infancy narrative of Luke's Gospel.

We can begin with Mary's song of praise, well known as the "Magnificat" (Lk. 1:46–55). This lowly peasant girl was told by the angel Gabriel that the child she would conceive would receive "the throne of his ancestor David. He will reign over the house of Jacob for ever, and of his kingdom there will be no end" (1:32–33). Clearly, then, this miracle involves God's remembering "the promise he made to our ancestors, to Abraham and to his descendants" (1:55). But what will happen as a result of the coming of the Messiah by the Holy Spirit? Mary anticipates that the powerful will be brought down and the lowly exalted, that the rich will be impoverished while the poor will be uplifted (1:52–53).

Zechariah, a faithful priest and husband of Elizabeth, Mary's relative, had already been told that his son, John (the Baptist), would "make ready a people prepared for the Lord" (1:17). On the day of John's circumcision (dedication), Zechariah confirms Mary's song through a prophecy from the Holy Spirit (1:67):

Blessed be the Lord God of Israel,
> for he has looked favorably on his people and
> redeemed them.
He has raised up a mighty savior for us
> in the house of his servant David,
as he spoke through the mouth of his holy prophets from of old,
> that we would be saved from our enemies and from the
> hand of all who hate us.

(1:68–71)

Zechariah also understood that the promised salvation of Israel would involve the peaceful forgiveness of their sins (1:78–79)—which necessarily had to precede the restoration of Israel—so he did not necessarily think that the messianic kingdom would involve a violent revolution. Nevertheless, God's redemption of Israel would shine a light on those who lived in the shadow of darkness and enable them once again to serve him in holiness and righteousness.

Last, when Jesus was presented in the temple, Simeon was said to be "looking forward to the consolation of Israel" (2:25) and Anna to be anticipating "the redemption of Jerusalem" (2:38). Under the inspiration of the Holy Spirit, Simeon comes to see that the consolation and restoration of Israel is necessarily intertwined with the fate of the rest of the world:

My eyes have seen your salvation,
>   which you have prepared in the presence of all peoples,
>   a light for revelation to the Gentiles
>   and for glory to your people Israel. (2:30–32)

Undoubtedly the prosperity of Israel depends on her restoration and living in peace with her Gentile neighbors.

Many contemporary readers have come to understand these references to the redemption of Israel in spiritual terms. After all, Jesus neither overthrew the Roman rule over Palestine nor established Yahweh's political reign over Israel. In fact, not only was the temple itself razed to the ground a generation later (in 70 CE), but there are other passages (to be discussed later) in Luke-Acts that seem to transfer the promises of the covenant from the Jews to the Gentiles.

But Jesus' birth is presented by Luke in terms that clearly announce his kingdom as being at least superimposed on if not replacing Caesar's. By the first century, Caesar's birthday was celebrated as symbolizing the "good news" that the emperor brought to his subjects throughout the empire, and Caesar was exalted as divine "Son of God," "lord," "redeemer," and "savior" through the cult of the emperor. Jesus is announced in precisely these terms as the "Son of the Most High" (Lk. 1:32) who would restore the Davidic kingdom. So if in those days even his parents were under the rule of king Herod of Judea and governor Quirinius of Syria, and even if they were subject to Augustus Caesar's decree of taxation, Jesus' birth brought forth the angelic proclamation regarding the arrival of "a Savior, who is the Messiah, the Lord" (2:11). Readers of the Gospel could hardly have missed Luke's understanding that Jesus' arrival challenged Caesar's assumed divinity, lordship, and salvific stature.

This background helps us to understand why the disciples, after following Jesus for three years and listening to him teach about the kingdom for forty days (Acts 1:3), still wondered if the times of restoration had finally arrived. If Jesus was the Messiah, then, according to the Old Testament—alluded to throughout Mary's Magnificat and Zechariah's prophecy—God was going to fulfill the covenant promises. Justice would be served on the enemies of Israel, on those powerful, proud, and rich Roman rulers and their aristocratic patrons (political, religious, and cultural leaders) who had conspired to keep the peasant farmworkers and landowners in poverty (through high taxation, sometimes of up to 50 percent of total crop) and thereby oppressed the lower classes. From the perspective of Mary, Joseph (a carpenter), and others at the bottom rung of Israelite society, the good news—the *euangelion*—of the Messiah's arrival brought with it tangible material expectations. If in fact Israel was to be saved from her enemies, God would have to raise up the Messiah to bring about a massive revolution.

Meanwhile, think for a moment about how the ruling classes of the first century might have reacted to news coming out of Palestine that the king long anticipated by the Jews had been born. What if they had heard that the kingdom of Jesus would be established over and against that of Caesar and his patrons and that part of the upheaval that would occur involved the leveling of the rich and powerful and the exaltation of the socially marginalized? Even if we grant for the moment that the kingdom proclaimed by Jesus was purely spiritual, the messianic expectations of the common people combined with the fears of the upper classes regarding the instability of their own social position would have been enough to cause a stir. Is it any wonder, then, that the Jewish religious leaders—groups like the chief priests, scribes, Pharisees, and

Sadducees that, unlike most modern political parties, were both religious and political—were concerned enough about how Jesus might upset their own place in the sociopolitical hierarchy that they led the charge eventually to execute him?

What is clear is that the promise to restore the kingdom was connected to the promise of the Holy Spirit. We shall see later that, just as the Holy Spirit worked in the life of Jesus to bring about the kingdom, so also the Spirit empowered his followers to herald the kingdom. What does this then say about us today who are recipients of the same Holy Spirit? Perhaps there is a middle ground between thinking either that the kingdom proclaimed by Jesus is a spiritual reality located in the coming future or that we are called to be revolutionaries who would overthrow the ruling empires of our world today. Maybe this middle ground involves our being open to receiving the Spirit's empowerment so that we also might be agents who hasten the kingdom, which is in some respects already present, even if it is in other respects still to come. Maybe it might involve our engaging with and dismantling, by the power of the Spirit, the unjust structures that keep the poor impoverished, as sung about by Mary. More unimaginably, maybe the Spirit will enable the reconciliation of enemies so that salvation would come upon traditional enemies, as Zechariah prophesied, but through just peacemaking rather than by the overthrow or annihilation of the historical adversaries. Why would it be impossible to imagine today, for example, peace between Jews and Palestinians, or between Israelis and Arabs? Is it not possible that the coming of the Spirit was intended to complete the work of restoring Israel but to do so precisely by including and reconciling Jews and Gentiles rather than by perpetuating their divisions? If so, then the promise to restore the kingdom is still in the making, by the power of the Holy Spirit.

3
Pentecost—the Spirit Poured Out on All Flesh!

Acts 2:1-21

*S*O THE DISCIPLES WENT OFF TO JERUSALEM, as instructed by Jesus, to await the arrival of the Holy Spirit. And the Holy Spirit did arrive, like a bang, on the Day of Pentecost, which was the traditional Feast of Weeks that occurred fifty days after the Feast of Passover (Lev. 23:15–21; Deut. 16:9–12) and that celebrated the wheat harvest as symbolic of the renewal of the Mosaic covenant. Little did they realize, however, the extent to which this Pentecost experience would contribute to the renewal of Israel.

The gift of the Spirit on this day marks the beginning of the fulfillment of the promise made to Abraham and repeated by Simeon: that the seed of Abraham would be the means through which the Gentiles would be blessed (Gen. 12:3; cf. Lk. 2:32). The covenant of God with Abraham, Moses, and David, in other words, was not only for the sake of Israel but also for the world. In the Pentecost event linguistic, ethnic, cultural, and national barriers between Israel and the Gentiles are overcome, making clear the universal scope of God's promises. To be sure, the goal of the Christian mission, as empowered by the Holy Spirit, was to take the gospel to the ends of the earth (Acts 1:8). Yet since the list of nations and peoples in this passage is representative of previous Jewish lists of nations— for example Genesis 10 and 1 Chronicles 1—the gift of the Holy

Spirit's outpouring on all those present on this day anticipates the outpouring on "all flesh" (Acts 2:17) that is to come.

The majority of those in Jerusalem were God-fearing and "devout Jews from every nation under heaven" (2:5). They certainly included Jews and Gentile proselytes to Judaism, but perhaps also partial converts who were uncircumcised or not fully Torah-observant. It seems likely that the original Christian community—the three thousand who were baptized in response to this Pentecost event (Acts 2:41)—inaugurated a new movement that included individuals with varying commitments to Jewish faith from around the Mediterranean world.

The mention of Cretans (2:11) would also have broken stereotypes about who was "in" or "out" of the kingdom, especially given the widespread belief, promulgated partly by Cretans themselves, that Cretans were "always liars, vicious brutes, lazy gluttons" (Titus 1:12). Clearly, the people swept up into this new Jesus movement included those who would have been excluded if the reigning prejudices of the day had been in effect. But imagine how different the history of the last two thousand years might have been if those from Arabia had been fully incorporated into the new people of God. Perhaps the split between the children of Sarah and Hagar, between the descendents of Jacob and Ishmael, might have been healed by the Spirit of reconciliation. Maybe contemporary hostilities in the Middle East would have been avoided if Jews, proselytes, or Gentiles from Arabia had nurtured the new relations brought about on the Day of Pentecost.

Is it possible that the Day of Pentecost restored the covenant promises to Israel in part by constituting a new people of God, one composed of Jews but yet not exclusive of proselytes and Gentiles, one that included a diversity of languages, and one that embodied a plurality of cultures and people groups? First-century Palestinian life, in many ways like our global village today, was marked by suspicions about those who were different, who spoke other languages, and who represented strange ways of life. It was the work of the Spirit, however, to overcome these barriers, to bring those who were strangers together, and to reconcile those who might have otherwise lived apart from those unlike themselves.

Pentecost thus inaugurates a restored Israel and God's kingdom by establishing new social structures and relations. Note that the gift of the Spirit was not withheld from any of the 120 men and women who had gathered in the upper room (Acts 1:14–15): the divided tongues of fire rested on each one and enabled each to either speak or be heard in foreign languages (2:3–4). In order to explain this phenomenon, Peter cites the prophet Joel:

> your sons and your daughters shall prophesy,
> and your young men shall see visions,
>   and your old men shall dream dreams.
> Even upon my slaves, both men and women,
>   in those days I will pour out my Spirit;
>   and they shall prophesy. (2:17–18; cf. Joel 2:28–29)

Peter clearly understood that, whereas the former Jewish era was patriarchal in character, the restoration of Israel would feature the equality of male and female: both would prophesy under the power of the Spirit. Whereas the former covenant featured the leadership of elders, the restored kingdom would involve the empowering of men and women of all ages. Whatever structures had previously sanctioned the social system of slavery, the outpouring of the Spirit had been and would be indiscriminately upon both free and slave, in effect making them equal. In all of this, the work of the Spirit was heralded in strange tongues, not the conventional languages of the status quo.

In effect, the restoration of the kingdom through the power of the Spirit actually overturned the status quo. As Mary and Zechariah had already foretold, those at the bottom of the social ladder—women, youth, and slaves—would be recipients of the Spirit and vehicles of the Spirit's empowerment. People previously divided by language, ethnicity, culture, nationality, gender, and class would be reconciled in this new version of the kingdom. Potentially, "all flesh" would be included within this kingdom of the last days (Acts 2:17).

Do these characteristics continue to mark the church as the fellowship of the Holy Spirit? Is the church still a universal presence that reconciles Jewish and Gentile communities divided for various reasons? Does the church still speak in the tongues of the Spirit that conjointly proclaim the renewal of Israel (thus preserving the distinctiveness of God's covenant with the Jews) and the introduction of the kingdom (thus opening up the promises of God to the world), or do we remain captive to the divisive languages, structures, and conventions of the empires of this world? Our prayer should be, "Come Holy Spirit!" so that the proclaimed outpouring of the Spirit on all flesh might indeed still find its fulfillment in our time.

PART TWO

The Power of the Spirit in Jerusalem

4
The Spirit's New Economy of Salvation

Acts 2:22-40

ETER'S QUOTATION FROM JOEL ends with the declaration that, on the glorious Day of the Lord when Yahweh would restore Israel, "everyone who calls on the name of the Lord shall be saved" (Acts 2:21). In that sense, the restoration of Israel involves the salvation both of the Jews and of all who call on the name of Yahweh. But there is more since, for Peter and Luke, who is retelling the history of Peter's sermon, salvation is bound up in "Jesus of Nazareth, a man attested to you by God with deeds of power, wonders, and signs that God did through him among you" (2:22). The heart of the Good News, then, was to "let the entire house of Israel know with certainty that God has made him both Lord and Messiah, this Jesus whom you crucified" (2:36).

We have already seen that the Jews were awaiting the Messiah, who would restore the house of Israel according to the promises made to Abraham, Moses, and David. Here in his first sermon, the Spirit-empowered Peter makes explicit Jesus' connections with the Davidic covenant. Not only does Peter mention David four times by name, but he also quotes or alludes to various royal psalms, songs that celebrate the restoration of the Davidic reign in the messianic age. One of these citations also confirms that Israel will be vindicated before her enemies (2:35; cf. Lk. 1:71; Ps. 110:1). The hope of the resurrection in ancient Israel was connected to the renewal of the Davidic covenant and the restoration of the nation (cf. Ezek. 37:1–14).

Luke is thereby accentuating Jesus' credentials in the line of David. But more than that, since David remained in the grave, Jesus is the one who fulfills the covenant promises about resurrection life. For the Jews who believed in a general raising of the dead at the end of the age connected with the restoration of Israel, the resurrection of Jesus would have meant both that David's kingship now belongs to Jesus and that the redemption of Israel and the last days, the Day of the Lord, had indeed arrived in the person of the man from Nazareth.

Further, the resurrection of Jesus precipitates his exaltation to the right hand of God from where, "having received from the Father the promise of the Holy Spirit, he has poured out this that you both see and hear" (Acts 2:33). So while the Father has promised the Spirit (Lk. 24:49), it is the resurrected Messiah who keeps the promise. Although salvation is based on the Spirit's work in and through the life, death, and resurrection of Lord Jesus (rather than Lord Caesar), it is realized and actualized through the ascended Messiah, who pours out that same Spirit on all flesh. If in the Gospel of Luke the Holy Spirit acts in the life of Jesus, in Acts, Jesus is present and active in the restored people of God in the power of the Spirit.

It is this exalted Messiah who has been crucified by a disbelieving and corrupt generation (2:40). Peter straightforwardly accuses his listeners, "You crucified and killed by the hands of those outside the law" (2:23; cf. 2:36). His audience is convicted by the fact that they have, however inadvertently, chosen to abide by the politics of Caesar and his lordship rather than that of the anointed Messiah. Wishing to avoid the judgment that befalls those who have executed an innocent man, they gasp, "What should we do?" (2:37). Peter responds: "Repent, and be baptized every one of you in the name of Jesus Christ so that your sins may be forgiven; and you will receive the gift of the Holy Spirit. For the promise is for you, for your children, and for all who are far away, everyone whom the Lord our God calls to him" (2:38–39).

Peter's response has drawn forth numerous interpretations during the two-thousand-year history of Christianity. I suggest that salvation consists not in emphasizing any one "thing," whether that be repentance, baptism, or the reception of the Spirit, but in repentance, baptism, the forgiveness of sins, and the receiving of the Holy Spirit *all together.* It must also be noted that forgiveness was originally a commercial notion that meant to be released from previous obligations and, in the first century, was also connected to the cleansing that had to occur in order for Israel to be renewed and restored.[2] So Peter's announcement offers his audience the forgiveness of sins committed by them and their ancestors, against one another and against God and his appointed Messiah—that is good news indeed, indicating the time had come for the restoration of Israel!

By extension, for the rest of us, forgiveness frees us from our indebtedness to others and allows us to receive a new identity, the gift of the Spirit, that transforms us into servants and friends of the Messiah. Yet such forgiveness and salvation cannot be magically earned by "fulfilling" this short list of requirements; rather, salvation involves God's calling, which enables repentance, God's acting in Christ to make possible the gracious forgiving of sins, and God's free outpouring, through Christ, of the Holy Spirit.

This mode of God's salvation involving the full scope of repentance, and the gift of the Holy Spirit seems to establish God's way of salvation once for all. That these promises are "for your children, and all who are far away" (2:39) points to both the spatial/geographical and the temporal reach of God's salvation: to those in the farthermost reaches of the empire or even Gentiles who would be at the ends of the earth (1:8) and to the many generations of descendants who shall call on the name of the Lord. In other words, if the powers and wonders of God accomplished in Jesus inaugurated the day of the Lord promised by the prophets, then the salvific plan of God outlined here in Peter's sermon will continue that work until the Day of the Lord, when the kingdom is fully present. So while the kingdom may be in the world, it is not of the world; rather, the coming kingdom that is the promise of the Father, the way of the Son, and the gift of the Holy Spirit is in the process of turning the kingdoms of this world "upside down" (17:6).

Now, Peter said much more than what Luke records. Nevertheless, this text raises many important questions. For example, what exactly does it mean that salvation introduces a new economy of grace, and how exactly does this get worked out while we remain within the economies of this world?

Let me suggest that the salvation of God overturns the economy of this world. Whereas the world's economic system depends on each one of us paying our debts, the economy of God's Spirit involves the forgiveness of debts. Whereas the world's justice system involves our getting what we earn or deserve, the justice of God liberates us from the guilt and shame accompanying our actions. Whereas our humanly constructed economy depends on barter and exchange, the divine economy involves merely calling on God in repentance and receiving both the forgiveness of debts and the free gift of the Holy Spirit. God's way of doing business is contrary to the ways of the world. Rather than merely meeting the obligations imposed by the law, the coming of the Trinitarian God establishes a new covenant of grace and a new economy of giving. The renewal of Israel, then, involves a kind of redemption that overthrows the rule (economy) of this world, albeit not precisely in the way that was expected.

5
Repentance as/and the Gift of the Holy Spirit

Luke 3:1-20; 19:1-10

ETER'S RESPONSE URGING REPENTANCE, baptism for the forgiveness of sins, and reception of the Holy Spirit may have been new to the crowd gathered on the Day of Pentecost. But it would not have surprised readers of Acts who had already read Luke's Gospel. Already in the wilderness ministry of John, they had been informed about his "proclaiming a baptism of repentance for the forgiveness of sins" (Lk. 3:3). Further, the ministry of the Baptist was to precipitate that of the Messiah as well as the coming of the Day of the Lord. Peter's interpretation of the events of the Day of Pentecost as related to the Spirit being poured out on all flesh so that "everyone who calls on the name of the Lord shall be saved" (2:21) did in fact fulfill the Isaianic promise regarding the ultimate result of John's ministry: that "all flesh shall see the salvation of God" (Lk. 3:6; cf. Isa. 40:3-4).

In response to John's prophetic preaching, the crowds of peasants and artisans who had flocked into the wilderness to hear him asked, "What then should we do?" (Lk. 3:10). John's response was very practical and concrete: "Whoever has two coats must share with anyone who has none; and whoever has food must do likewise" (3:11). For these subsistence farmers and others who lived on the underside of Roman society, receiving a coat or a meal may have meant the difference between making it from one day to the next. Repentance, therefore, was not just an abstract idea but also a concrete way of relating to those who were otherwise thought to be one's competitors for the same scarce resources. This sort of repentance and associated forgiveness would mark the emergence of a renewed Israel, according to the promises of God.

Among the crowds were also the despised tax collectors and imperial guard. Most of these would have been Jews who were paid to work for the political, religious, and social hierarchy. So they would have been seen as having betrayed their own people since they made their living at the expense of those in the lower classes. John's preaching also moved them to repentance, and he straightforwardly insisted that the tax collectors should "collect no more than the amount prescribed for you," and the soldiers should "not extort money from anyone by threats or false accusation, and be satisfied with your wages" (3:13–14). The marks of genuine repentance would be manifest in concrete acts of honesty, uprightness, and hospitality. When performed, these countercultural responses would produce true descendents of Abraham (3:8), reconcile them with their estranged fellow Israelites, and renew the covenant promises of God.

The message of John's ministry is clearly seen and extended in the ministry of Jesus. Luke later tells of Zacchaeus, the rich "*chief* tax-collector" (19:2, my emphasis), and his encounter with Jesus. Whether motivated out of repentance or the need to defend his actions before a hostile crowd, Zacchaeus said, "Half of my possessions, Lord, I will give to the poor; and if I have defrauded anyone of anything, I will pay back four times as much" (19:8). Now, as Zacchaeus' fourfold repayment met the most exacting rather than the minimal demands of the law (compare Exod. 22:1 with Lev. 6:5; Num. 5:7), this brought forth Jesus' declaration,

"Today salvation has come to this house, because he too is a son of Abraham" (Lk. 19:9). Zacchaeus' willingness to make amends not only brings him back into fellowship with the people whom he had swindled but also in effect saves, restores, and renews a community torn apart by greed, distrust, and strife. If too many tax collectors had repented of their sins like Zacchaeus and become reconciled with the people, they would cease to be cheats, and that in turn would undermine the imperial economy that favored the elite.

In other words, the message of repentance and baptism for the forgiveness of sins preached by both John (in Luke) and Peter (in Acts) heals communities, reconciles those otherwise alienated from one another, and renews the covenant made with Israel even while it threatens to overthrow the systems of this world. Thus in John's case, the people's hearts were "filled with expectation, and all were questioning . . . whether he might be the Messiah" (Lk. 3:15). Perhaps they still thought it was impossible to produce these acts of repentance apart from the full restoration of the messianic kingdom. John's response was that the Messiah would come and "baptize you with the Holy Spirit and fire" (3:16).

On the Day of Pentecost, the promised Messiah had visited his people with tongues of fire and of the Spirit. Those who received the power of the Spirit were able to bear witness to a repented life of mutual sharing of all things (Acts 2:45). In short, the restoration of the kingdom would involve the "fruits worthy of repentance" (Lk. 3:8) as made possible through the gift of the Holy Spirit.

The political dimensions of John's preaching should not be overlooked. At the end of this passage, Luke mentions that John was imprisoned by Herod, and later we are told he was beheaded by Herod, who was upset that John had rebuked him for taking his brother's wife, Herodias, as his own. But Luke also clearly says that John fearlessly castigated Herod "because of all the evil things that Herod had done" (3:19). Even if we are not told what these evils consisted of (Herod of Galilee, also known as Herod Antipas, should not be confused with Herod the Great, his father, who reigned over Judea when Jesus and John were born and issued the edict to slaughter the infants around Bethlehem), it is safe to conjecture that John's preaching threatened the very fabric of the Roman Empire as it had been construed in Palestine at that time.

Here was a revolutionary message, one that urged the masses to shift their allegiances from Caesar to the coming Messiah and that was characterized not only by changes in hearts but also by changed lives. If the imperial economy was predicated on the patronage of the aristocratic elite, dependent on the power of the imperial army, and turned on the dishonesty of the empire's collection agents, then the new messianic economy emphasized giving rather than hoarding or taking, honesty instead of cheating or extortion, and uprightness rather than lawlessness and false allegations. So whereas the salvation wrought by Caesar was enjoyed only by the elite few who betrayed the trust of the masses, the salvation of the Messiah would baptize all who called on the name of the Lord into a new economy marked by forgiveness of sins and debts and a new community, the restored Israel and the reconstituted people of God.

Genuine repentance would precipitate the renewal of God's people. It would bring about new relationships, interactions, and exchanges, and this would inspire the people who labored under Roman rule toward a wholly new form of life. It is not only Herod of Galilee who is threatened but also the entire imperial hierarchy as represented by Tiberius (the second Roman emperor, from 14 to 37 CE); Pontius Pilate of Judea (who governed from 26 to 36 CE);

Herod's brother Philip (who ruled over Ituraea and Trachonitis from 4 BCE to 34 CE); Lysanias (who reigned in Abilene, north of Galilee, from 28 to ca. 37 CE); and the religious-political leadership represented by Annas and Caiaphas (all mentioned in 3:1–2). No wonder those who saw Jesus accept Zaccheus grumbled that "he has gone to be the guest of one who is a sinner" (19:7). Discerning observers would have foreseen that the preaching of the baptism of repentance and forgiveness of sins would dismantle the imperial hierarchy, overturn the class system, and upset the existing state of affairs. It was not without reason, then, that the political powers executed the Baptist and the religious elites followed suit later with his cousin.

One question for us today, especially we who are on the top side of the global market economy, is whether we would do any different: would we embrace and then live out the "good news" of the coming kingdom or would we fight to preserve the status quo and our own place in it? If the Holy Spirit were to convict our hearts like Zaccheus's, our response just might also extend the new economy of salvation so as to reconcile people, oppose and correct the unjust structures of our world, and bring about the healing of many nations.

6
Fellowship in the Spirit

Acts 2:41-47

S O WHAT EXACTLY HAPPENED when the crowd of three thousand who heard Peter repented, were baptized in Jesus' name for the forgiveness of sins, and received the Holy Spirit? They were being saved! But this salvation had to do not only with what happened after they died but also marked the continuing work of God in the Messiah to redeem Israel. If John and Jesus both called the Jews to repentance, the miracle of Pentecost may have been that the restoration of Israel had expanded to include Gentile converts to Judaism as well. These messianic Jews and proselytes gathered from day to day in the temple (2:46) in anticipation of the full restoration of the holy site to the people of God, as had been promised to David.

Yet while awaiting the full consummation of Israel, the renewed people of God "devoted themselves to the apostles' teaching and fellowship, to the breaking of bread and the prayers. . . . All who believed were together and had all things in common; they would sell their possessions and goods and distribute the proceeds to all, as any had need. Day by day . . . they broke bread at home and ate their food with glad and generous hearts" (2:42, 44–46). Now recall that the crowd that had gathered in Jerusalem had come from around the Mediterranean world for the Feast of Pentecost. Maybe some of the three thousand were residents (not counting the original 120 who had gathered together in the upper room), but most were probably visitors, perhaps with relatives in the area. Still, one can imagine how this mass acknowledgment of the messiahship of Jesus must have forced the apostles to scramble to organize a viable form of communal life that would not only meet the needs of the people but also serve the purposes of discipleship. The latter involved teaching, fellowship, the breaking of bread, and prayers. Perhaps the breaking of bread referred to here was an extension of the rite instituted by Jesus at the Last Supper, but one whose full significance the apostolic community had yet to comprehend. It occurred daily in the various homes through the sharing of meals but may also have been practiced in the temple.

Note also that the repentance and forgiveness of debts preached by John, Jesus, and Peter are lived out in a very concrete manner. The people shared what they had, and the more affluent sold whatever was necessary in order to meet the needs of others in the community. Here the example set by Zaccheus seems to have been multiplied many times over. The "glad and generous hearts" (2:46) of the people reflect their living in simplicity and liberality rather than being calculative and self-seeking. Such communal practices by these early followers of Jesus persisted for a while (see Acts 4:32–37), although we do not know for how long. It's clear, however, that those who had repented and were baptized in the name of Jesus for the forgiveness of sins saw themselves as being called to embody the Way of life exemplified by Messiah Jesus and experienced and taught by his closest disciples. The restoration of Israel was no mere spiritual event; instead, the outpouring of the Holy Spirit by the ascended Jesus established a new communal body that provided an alternative form of life to that under the lordship of Caesar.

Don't confuse this early Jewish-Christian way of life with some sort of socialism or communism. Karl Marx's critiques were directed at the industrialism he saw in mid-nineteenth-century England, when workers were forced to sell their labor at the market rate (which was then insufficient to supply their daily needs) and then not allowed to keep their profits (which were pocketed by the capitalist merchants). Marx's solution was to distribute both private property and the ownership of productive capital to the proletariat (workers) so that they could gain from the profits of their labor.

What happened among the three thousand converts on the Day of Pentecost was not an early expression of Marx's manifesto. For one thing, the sharing of these early followers of Jesus as the Messiah was motivated by a repentant heart and the gift of the Holy Spirit, not by the socialist rule of law. For this reason, the selling of personal possessions was a voluntary practice rather than an institutionalized rejection of private property. Further, such sale and distribution of proceeds did not seem to have occurred systematically; instead, this unfolded over time, according to the needs of the community. What Luke describes here is not some early form of communism but is exemplary of the community of the Holy Spirit.

At the same time, this early apostolic community embodied values about fellowship (*koinōnia;* 2:42), mutual empathy, and solidarity that are also a far cry from what we today call free-market capitalism. If life in the Spirit liberates the people of God in ways that counter the oppressive and stifling regimes that have typically marked Communist societies, so also does the fellowship of the Spirit call into question the greed, consumerism, materialism, and militarism that characterize much of life amid today's neoliberal market economy. How might the example of the early community of the Spirit challenge our own complicity in the practices that sustain and perpetuate inequities in the global village? What does it mean for us to resist the systemic forces that oppress the poor and to do so according to the model presented by the early followers of Jesus? Is it possible to translate this model of life under grace and include the forgiveness of debts in twenty-first-century middle-class America and the capitalist order of the global market?

I think we must recognize that the practices of the kingdom represent a contrast to both Communism and capitalism as we understand these today. Rather than either having to sell our work for the profits of others or having to redistribute the fruits of our labor through a socialist system, perhaps the gift of the Holy Spirit empowers us to give not out of our own need but out of the abundance of God. The divine economy of grace meets the needs of all neither through the "invisible hand" of the free market nor the enforced regime of a socialist economy but rather through the mutuality and reciprocity of the fellowship birthed out of the messianic gift of the Spirit. The salvation promised through repentance, baptism, and the gift of the Holy Spirit liberates the people of God from alienation from God, from others, and even from the products of their labor, since we are no longer held in bondage to "what is ours" (or mine!). We are empowered to have all things in common and to give as each one has need.

We see that Peter and the apostles took his words seriously: they repented of their sins, received forgiveness, and extended forgiveness to others in ways that brought about the emergence of a new Israel, a new community of those who lived according to Jesus' kingdom message. It was this early community that revealed the significant implications of repentance, baptism, and the forgiveness of sins in a fallen world like the one we live in. Such "salvation" was not merely spiritual but consisted of a gospel—Good News—to be lived out. People now lived differently who were really baptized with the Holy Spirit and with fire!

7

The Mission of Jesus Christ, the Anointed One

Luke 4:14-30

I F THE IMAGE OF THE NONHIERARCHICAL FELLOWSHIP OF EQUALS just portrayed seems far-fetched, perhaps we are judging it not according to life in the power of the Spirit but according to our own twenty-first-century middle-class biases and presuppositions. Let's continue to interrogate our own assumptions on these matters by attending further to Luke's narrative of the life and ministry of Jesus.

Luke 4:14–30 records the beginning of Jesus' public ministry in his hometown of Nazareth and his home region of Galilee. Jesus begins his ministry "filled with the power of the Spirit" (4:14). In recognition of the anointing that is upon him, he announces, from the messianic text of the prophet Isaiah (61:1–2),

> The Spirit of the Lord is upon me,
>> because he has anointed me to bring good news to the poor.
> He has sent me to proclaim release to the captives
>> and recovery of sight to the blind, to let the oppressed go free,
> to proclaim the year of the Lord's favour. (Lk. 4:18–19)

Rather than seeing each of these as separate elements of Jesus' messianic vocation, we should view them instead as interrelated aspects of his mission to restore the covenant to Israel. In this regard we need to keep in mind the following.

To begin with, the poor, the captives, the blind, and the oppressed are neither merely metaphors nor to be applied only to four literal groups of people. The former interpretation would spiritualize these labels, but that would ignore the fact that Jesus' public ministry in the rest of the Gospel narrative actually did release captives, open blind eyes, and liberate the oppressed. The latter interpretation might lead us to think that the "Good News" was limited to four types of people groups.

Instead, we should see these references as including the broad spectrum of inhabitants among the lower classes of first-century Palestine. These were folk who were actually poor, blind, and oppressed, and Jesus' ministry was to and for them. In addition, there were others like lepers, the spiritually impoverished (including tax collectors such as Zaccheus), and the demonically oppressed to whom the gospel was directed. All of these were people of low, no, or despicable status in Greco-Roman society—which constituted about 95 percent of the population, who lived under the yoke of the imperial government, the religious-social elite, and the landed aristocracy—and it was to these poor that the messianic message was particularly relevant.

From this perspective, the messianic ministry is good news in very concrete ways. To the blind, it meant the opening of eyes and the gift of vision (see Lk. 7:21–22; 18:35–42); to those in captivity or who were oppressed, it meant deliverance, often understood in terms of liberation from demonic oppression; and to the poor, it meant their release from captivity or even indebtedness (the word "release" being the same word that is also translated "forgiveness"). With these elements combined, the Spirit-anointed ministry of Jesus would bring about "the year of the Lord's favour" (4:19).

Understood according to the messianic promises of the Hebrew prophets, including that of Isaiah, who is being quoted in this passage, this "year of the Lord" would have been taken as a reference to the Year of Jubilee announced in the Torah.[3] There were three key features of the Jubilee year (the fiftieth year after seven cycles of seven years): (1) that debts would be canceled; (2) that slaves would be freed; and (3) that land would be returned to its original owners. Jesus' pronouncement that "today this scripture has been fulfilled in your hearing" (4:21) was therefore greeted with joy by his listeners, those on the underside of society.

Jesus' public ministry did not in any straightforward sense result in a literal implementation of the Jubilee program. However, the establishment of the early messianic community (Acts 2:42–47) did create an alternative mode of life that instituted the spirit if not the letter of the Jubilee prescriptions. While we are not explicitly told that economic debts were canceled, we have already seen that the socioeconomic system was radically restructured in the apostolic community precisely in order to provide relief for the needy. Just as important, the declaration of the forgiveness of sins renewed the covenant with Israel and created a radically egalitarian community in the sense in which all were acknowledged sinners before God but yet were absolved and exonerated of their wrongdoings, and hence equally accepted in the fellowship of the Spirit.

The early messianic community understood that Jesus' proclamation of good news to the poor was intended to accomplish the renewal of Israel and the establishment of the kingdom (the year of the Lord's favor). Because the power of the same Spirit who anointed Jesus had been poured out on them, the disciples realized that their lives would be an extension of the ministry of Jesus.

Fast-forward, then, to today. Shouldn't we embrace the anointing of the Spirit in our lives by following in the footsteps of the disciples? The power of the Spirit is present now also to enable us to bring good news to the poor and to live out the gospel for the oppressed and those in captivity. This would involve not only declaring to the poor that their sins are forgiven, and not only feeding, clothing, and providing for the poor, as important as that might be. But it may also involve doing what the early messianic believers did: restructuring our very lives and communities so that the lines between the haves and the have-nots are overcome, so that none should be in need!

Note also how Jesus attempts to lead his followers to see the year of the Lord's favor as being not just for them as Jews but also for others as well. In a sense, the crowd was saying that, if the year of the Lord had truly arrived, then why had Jesus not accomplished more of the messianic works in the city of Nazareth in particular and the region of Galilee in general (Lk. 4:23)? Jesus' response drew from the ministries of Elijah and Elisha: that one was sent to a Gentile widow (the area of Sidon was outside of Jewish territory at that time) while the other was sent to a Syrian leper. If the anointing of the Spirit meant good news to the poor, such was not limited to the Jews. Rather, the gospel of the kingdom was also for Gentiles, including those at the lowest sectors of the social world: women, widows, lepers, and the impure.

With this saying, not even Jesus' initial warm reception by the Galileans could keep him in good stead with the local Nazarene synagogue leaders and members. They "were filled with rage" (4:28) and attempted to kill him. (Somehow, Jesus escaped to continue the work of restoring the kingdom, but only for a brief period of time.) Sometimes perhaps we are like those self-righteous Nazarenes who thought of themselves as deserving the presence and power of the Holy Spirit but not others who are beyond the scope of God's redemptive love.

8
The Holy Spirit and the Politics of Healing

Acts 3:1-4:31

*J*ESUS' PERSECUTION AT NAZARETH that we just saw fore-shadowed the persecution that the disciples would experience as a result of ministering in his name. In fact, his life provided a model for the ministry of his disciples.

Thus, just as Jesus was sent to the poor—understood as those being on the margins and underside of history—so also in the first episode of the disciples' ministry the leading apostles were sent to such an individual. This unnamed man's poverty, however, was explicitly linked to his disability: he had been lame for over forty years, from the time of his birth (Acts 3:2; 4:22). According to the Jewish understanding of the law, then, this man's disability was probably the result of sin in the lives of his parents or ancestors (compare Jn. 9:2 and Deut. 28:15–68). In one sense, he was deserving of his lot in life, and his lameness in effect marked him as being one who was outside the covenant promises of Yahweh. Here was one who was doubly oppressed, and his place was outside the temple (cf. Lev. 21:17–20).

But the power of the Spirit who worked through Jesus to open the eyes of the blind and heal the lame was also present with Peter and John. With Jesus at the right hand of the Father, the anointing of the Spirit accomplished the healing of the lame man in Jesus' name

(Acts 3:6, 16). As a result, this one whose disability had kept him from entering the temple courts was vindicated, and he approached the inner sanctuary by jumping, leaping, and praising God (3:8–9).

This healing of the lame man should not be seen as an isolated act of mercy but as part of the wider messianic task of restoring Israel and ushering in the great and glorious year of the Lord's favor, especially for those on the underside of history. In fact, the prophets had foretold that in the redeeming year of Yahweh, "the lame shall leap like a deer" (Isa. 35:6)!

As such, Peter understood the manifest presence of Jesus through the Spirit as an occasion to once again invite the crowd of Israelites to repent and receive the forgiveness of sins (3:12, 19). But what Jesus had implied to the Nazarenes in the synagogue Peter now explicitly declares: "That times of refreshing may come from the presence of the Lord, and that he may send the Messiah appointed for you, that is, Jesus, who must remain in heaven until the time of universal restoration that God announced long ago through his holy prophets" (3:20–21). In other words, the restoration of Israel was somehow connected to the renewal of all things to God, even though (as we shall see later in Acts 10) Peter himself did not fully understand the implications of this redemptive work of God at this time.

Now just as it was the religious leaders of Nazareth (initially) who persecuted Jesus, so also it was the religious leaders of Jerusalem (initially) who persecuted the disciples. But more specifically, it was the same group of religio-political leaders—"Annas the high priest, Caiaphas, John, and Alexander, and all who were of the high-priestly family" (compare Acts 4:6 with Lk. 3:2 and Jn. 18:13–24)—who participated in the trial and crucifixion of Jesus not too long ago that now led the inquisition against the apostles. Of course there were others, particularly the party of the Sadducees, who did not believe in the possibility of resurrection and who probably took issue with the theological claims of Peter regarding Jesus' having been raised from the dead (Acts 4:1–2). However, we should not underestimate the concerns of the Jewish leadership that all of this preaching about the lordship and messiahship of Jesus (3:20) threatened to overthrow the religio-political hierarchy, close to the top at which they themselves were perched.

Interested with preserving their place on the social, political, and economic ladder, the religious hierarchy was very much worried about the power and authority they saw manifest in the apostolic preaching and that was drawing thousands into a new way of life right there in Jerusalem. Their worst fears seemed to be unfolding: they had, with the help of the Romans, put to death the man from Nazareth who preached about the year of the Lord's favor, did the works of the kingdom, and also gathered together thousands of followers; but his message and deeds had now reappeared among his uneducated companions. It was precisely in Jesus' name that the lame man was healed, and only in and through his name—not in Caesar's!—that such healing and redemption (salvation) was being declared to all under heaven (4:10, 12).

It is important here to follow the cue provided by Luke to note that "salvation" in Luke and Acts almost never refers primarily to what happens after death, but means, literally, wholeness and health. The healing of this man involved not only the cure of his lameness but also his reintegration into Jewish communal life as represented by his entering the temple. Further, he would no longer be a beggar but could now make contributions as a member of his society. In each of these ways, the good news of salvation had relevance not for the afterlife but for life in the here and now.

In addition, just like the healings Jesus accomplished, the healing of the lame man at the Beautiful Gate turned out to have potentially drastic political implications. The politics of healing did not just expose the unbelief of the religious leadership; more disconcertingly, for those interested in preserving the class system, which kept the masses trampled under the aristocratic and imperial foot, the apostolic community recognized and proclaimed that the religious hierarchy was interwoven with the political authorities, and both were dependent on the mechanisms of the other. If the authorities had been privy to the prayers of the persecuted community, they would have known the followers of Jesus recognized only one "Sovereign Lord, who made the heaven and the earth, the sea, and everything in them" (4:24), and that they linked the unbelief of the Jewish leaders to the unbelief of the imperial government and vice versa:

> Why did the Gentiles rage,
>> and the peoples imagine vain things?
> The kings of the earth took their stand,
>> and the rulers have gathered together
> against the Lord and against his Messiah.
> (4:25–26; cf. Ps. 2:1–2)

Even amid persecution, the fledgling messianic community pleaded for more boldness, more healings, and more signs and wonders (4:30–31), and perhaps even their opponents sensed that these prayers were being heard.

So just as the religious leadership and imperial authorities had refused to believe in the messianic proclamation of Jesus, so also did they now persecute those who preached the restoration of the kingdom in Jesus' name. Just as the powers that be had preferred their dishonesty and unrighteousness (at the expense of the masses) over the ways of the messianic kingdom, so also did these same powers now resort to the worldly mechanisms of political threats (4:17–21), precisely that which the soldiers under John's ministry had forsaken (Lk. 3:14). Rather than embracing the Day of the Lord's favor offered by Peter (Acts 2:21), the religious hierarchy preferred the lordship of Caesar. Their culpability is now emphasized as intertwined with that of the Gentile imperium: "For in this city, in fact, both Herod and Pontius Pilate, with the Gentiles and the peoples of Israel, gathered together against your holy servant Jesus" (4:27). The other difference now was that it was the thousands of servants of Jesus, "filled with the Holy Spirit" and with boldness (4:8, 31), who were threatening to overturn the status quo.

We should also understand healing today not just as a salvific event (which it is, for those who are sick) but as also having a political dimension. Consider for instance advances in medicine. While we should not dismiss the responsible use of medicine, we can come to rely on that more than on God's power to heal. Better instead to view medicine as part of God's means of healing, even as we recognize that God may in some instances choose to accomplish such purposes quite apart from conventional medical means. More important, and more complicated, is the fact that our health-care systems in this world are interwoven with complicated economic and political structures (e.g., as manifest in the congressional debates regarding health insurance). In short, if we are to view the opening of blind eyes and the strengthening of lame legs as signs of the arrival of the new age of the kingdom, then we must also take political and economic measures to make such medical means accessible to as many as possible. Only then will the manifest healing power of the Spirit announce more unambiguously the establishment of the lordship of Jesus the Christ that will put an end to the kingdoms of this world.

9
Charismatic Healing as a Sign of the Kingdom

Luke 5:12-26; 6:6-11; 7:1-10; 8:40-56

S WE JUST SAW, the healing of the man at the Beautiful Gate involved the political intrigue surrounding all of Jesus' healing acts. Now, in the Lukan passages under consideration in this chapter (which are meant to be a representative rather than exhaustive collection of Jesus' healings in the Gospel), six miraculous cures are recorded. I suggest that these charismatic healings of Jesus, accomplished through him by the power of the Holy Spirit, are signs of the year of the Lord's favor (Lk. 4:19) and of the kingdom, and in that sense have sociopolitical dimensions that are often overlooked. This is a place where you will really need to have your New Testament close at hand—to join me in looking closely at these passages in Luke's Gospel. Let's see how these healings are both embedded in deeper social, political, and religious structures while they also herald the redemption and transformation of these realities in light of the coming reign of God.

To begin, Jesus cleanses a leper (Lk. 5:12–15). Leprosy in the ancient world was not just a skin condition; rather, it required the kind of social quarantine that effectively removed lepers from their homes, families, and communities. There were extensive provisions made under the Mosaic law with regard to the diagnosis, treatment, and purification of lepers and their dwelling places (Lev. 13–14). So when Jesus touched this man, he transgressed the biblical, legal, medical, and social conventions of his time. Yet Jesus knew that the social dimensions of leprosy had to be explicitly addressed, even though the man had been healed. Thus he instructs the man to "go . . . and show yourself to the priest, and, as Moses commanded, make an offering for your cleansing, for a testimony to them" (Lk. 5:14). The miracle would have been incomplete on its own apart from the socioreligious act through which the priest declared the man cleansed and fit to be reintegrated into the community.

This pericope is followed immediately by the story of the paralytic who was let down through a roof by his friends into the presence of Jesus (Lk. 5:17–26). While Luke suggests that the man was unable to see Jesus because of the crowds, in contemporary parlance this paralyzed or bedridden man had a problem with accessibility. Jesus' healing is intertwined with his pronouncement of forgiveness of sins. While we have already seen that forgiveness of sins involves the release from all debts and necessarily precedes the renewal of Israel, in this case, Jesus' pronounced absolution also with regard to God (5:20–21). Declaration of the forgiveness of sins served not only existential and therapeutic functions but also spiritual and theological ones related to this man's physical healing. Healing is therefore a sign, not only of the power of God to restore human bodies, but also of Jesus as representative of the messianic promise to bring about the redemption, reconciliation, and release long associated with the year of the Lord's favor.

Just as important is that Jesus healed this man because he knew he was surrounded by Pharisees and teachers of the law (5:17). This is the first time in Luke's Gospel that the Pharisees are mentioned.

In questioning Jesus' authority to forgive sins (5:21), the Pharisees no doubt were also expressing skepticism that this was the one who would renew and restore Israel. The healing of this paralytic highlighted the interconnections between healing and forgiveness. More importantly, it located Jesus' mighty works squarely in the public sphere of Jewish social and religious life and signaled to the people (and their religious leaders) that God was present in this man to accomplish the redemption of Israel. From this moment on in the Gospel of Luke, hostilities between Jesus and the religious leaders intensify.

The next healing, that of the man with a withered hand (Lk. 6:6–11), takes place in the synagogue on the Sabbath. Luke has just told of Jesus' violation of Sabbath laws before his Pharisaic inter-rogators (6:1–5). Again, Jesus knows he is being watched and yet says to the man, "Come and stand here" (6:8), thereby ensuring that his interactions with the man are done in plain sight. While his opponents are looking to bring accusations against him, Jesus asks them, "Is it lawful to do good or to do harm on the sabbath, *to save life* or to destroy it?" (6:9, my italics). Jesus turns the tables by linking the purposes of the Sabbath with the saving interventions of God. In order to fulfill the divine intentions for the Sabbath rest, then, Jesus accomplishes God's salvific work not by forgiving his sins but by restoring the withered hand. So, although the Jews believed in Yahweh as Savior, they were unprepared for Yahweh's manifestation in the form of Jesus. Instead Jesus' appearance as the mediator of divine salvation (cf. 1:47; 2:11) infuriated the scribes and Pharisees (6:11).

The salvation of God is hereby also interrelated with the Sabbath rest established to ensure that human rhythms are brought into sync with those of God's creation. The salvation manifest in this healing is a sign of the coming kingdom, which fulfills God's intentions to bring about the shalom of the Sabbath.

The next two healings highlight that, while in general Jesus directed his ministry to the poor underclass of Palestinian society, he also interacted with the ruling elite when opportunities presented themselves. Both the centurion at Capernaum (Lk. 7:1–2) and Jairus, the leader of the synagogue (7:41), were patrons who served as brokers between the imperial government and the masses. The centurion's elite status is clearly identified as is his being a benefactor for the Jews in terms of his love for them and his having built their synagogue (7:5). (First-century patrons were those like the centurion who provided goods and services for their clients, who in turn incurred debts of loyalty to their sponsor.) While he was in a position to make demands of lower-class carpenters such as Jesus, the centurion recognized Jesus' authority and acted deferentially toward him—first by sending friends to intercept Jesus and then by not being presumptive regarding Jesus (7:6–7). But even as the centurion contravened the social conventions of his time by acting more like a client than a patron, Jesus in turn also seemed intent on breaking social expectations by entering into the home of a Gentile (7:6). Then Jesus expresses amazement at the centurion's faith and accomplishes the healing of the slave. In short, this narrative is less about the healed slave than it is about the promises of God to extend the covenant to the Gentiles. This anticipates the expansion of the gospel to Cornelius in Acts even as it locates the healing power of God amid the social and political domains of human lives.

The healing of Jairus's daughter (Lk. 8:40–42, 49–56) further reveals the social implications of God's saving actions. The restoration of the girl occurs only after an interruption involving a hemorrhaging woman. Yet Jesus explicitly defines this resuscitation as being salvific: "Do not fear. Only believe, and she will be saved" (8:50). The salvation of the girl was also eminently that of her family's. Jesus' directing the parents to give their daughter something to eat (8:55) symbolizes not only the life-giving nourishment of food but also the life-sustaining practices of eating together as a social activity. Both cases involving Jairus and the centurion, then, reveal how their encounters with Jesus brought about a transformation of the normal patron-client relations that governed first-century interactions between religious and military elites and their clientele.

Last for our purposes but not least with regard to Jesus' healing acts is the woman who had been hemorrhaging (and therefore was unclean) for twelve years and had been reduced to penury. These "three strikes"—being a woman, unclean, and poor—did not discourage her from pressing up against the crowd to touch Jesus, during the process of which her defiled status rendered ritually impure all she came into contact with. As with the leper we saw above, her physical healing was incomplete apart from Jesus' socially confirming her cleansing. The interchange that followed resulted in a threefold affirmation (8:48), countering the "three strikes": her dignity and status were restored in Jesus' addressing her as a "daughter" (of Abraham; cf. 1:55); she was physically healed but now also socially redeemed and made well (whole); and she was given the gift of peace not only in terms of her physical condition but also in terms of her now being accepted when she had heretofore been rejected and marginalized. This public acknowledgment was an essential component to Jesus' healing given the woman's "sin" of contaminating the crowd because of her hemorrhaging condition.

We have no space to explore the many other healings of Jesus recorded in the Gospel of Luke. My primary point in all of this discussion is to highlight the wider social and political significance of the healing acts of Jesus. In each case the healings are signs announcing the in-breaking of God's kingdom, whether in terms of release from sins or debts, reconciliation with the community, restoration of social dignity, or the reordering of sociopolitical relations. Jesus' healings performed other functions besides mending broken bodies; they both heralded the final restoration of Israel even as they constituted the arrival of the ultimate Sabbath rest. Against this background it is less of a wonder that the apostolic healings in Jesus' name later on (e.g., in Acts) both participated in the ushering in of the day of the Lord's favor and simultaneously elicited the kinds of hostile reactions from the religious leaders expressed previously against Jesus himself.

Stepping back into our present, then, we should reflect on the fact that there is more to divine healing than biomedical intervention. As socio-psycho-somatic wholes, our health requires both physical curing as well as psychospiritual remediation, including reconciliation with God. Human beings are sociopolitical and economic creatures such that holistic health also involves resolution of interpersonal relationships, reintegration into communities, and restoration of human self-worth vis-à-vis the perceptions of others. Insofar as Western medicine bifurcates our bodies from the rest of us, it can only fix some of our symptoms but cannot bring about full healing; our best medicinal practices remain but partial signs of the kingdom. What might Spirit-empowered followers of Jesus do today to redeem and transform our health-care systems at all levels—medicine, accessibility, insurance, and so on—so that healing could once again herald the year of the Lord?

The charismatic healings of Jesus were signs of the kingdom precisely because Jesus refused to fall in line with the social conventions of his day. He repeatedly crossed social, religious, and theological boundaries—touching lepers, forgiving sins, declaring the impure to be clean, interacting with Israel's patrons unlike a client, and so on—as he acted under the Holy Spirit's empowerment to announce and establish the day of the Lord. While there were some of the ruling hierarchy who were open to embracing Jesus' new world order, most of the religious leaders, landed aristocracy, and imperial elite would have felt threatened about losing their place in the social system.

Are we today fully committed to the kind of whole and transformative community that is the reign of God, and if so how might our actions be subversive of current ruling powers? If we are not caught up with maintaining our own place in the social order, we could become better agents of the charismatic power of the Spirit to bring about the healing signs of the coming kingdom.

PART THREE

The Economics of the Spirit in Judea

10
Economics of the Spirit

Acts 4:32-5:11

*T*HERE ARE OTHER PASSAGES IN ACTS that reveal other reasons why the religious and political leaders of Palestine had become concerned about the fledgling Christian community in Jerusalem. Within a short time there were over five thousand members from around the area and the wider Mediterranean world gathered around the apostles (Acts 4:4; there were already at least that many Judean followers of Jesus during the time of his public ministry—see Lk. 9:14). While these included some landowners and those from the wealthier upper classes, the apostolic leaders also had to ensure that the needs of the poorest in their midst were being met. What was emerging was a fully mutual (rather than hierarchical) community in which "those who believed were of one heart and soul, and no one claimed private ownership of any possessions, but everything they owned was held in common" (Acts 4:32). Not only were the more affluent willing to share with those less privileged, but even the poor had internalized the message of Jesus to them (in "the Sermon on the Plain") to give, share, and lend to one another without expectation of repayment (Lk. 6:30–35). This kind of alternative way of life enacted on a large scale would surely threaten the social, economic, and political pyramids of power that served the purposes of the urban elite at the expense of the masses below.

In fact, it was out of the matrix of such communal selflessness and mutuality that the apostolic testimony to Jesus proceeded with such power. Whereas earlier it was said of the apostolic community that it elicited "the goodwill of all the people" (Acts 2:47), here it is clear that the community was pleasing to God, who in turn bestowed "great grace . . . upon them all" (4:33). The apostolic proclamation made the impression it did precisely because their love for God was backed up with and manifested by their concrete love for one another. The fulfillment of the greatest commandment involved loving God and neighbor (Lk. 10:25–28). Jesus said, "I give you a new commandment, that you love one another. Just as I have loved you, you also should love one another. By this everyone will know that you are my disciples, if you have love for one another" (Jn. 13:34–35).

The resurrection of Jesus was therefore not just talked about but witnessed to in tangible deeds of selfless sharing so that "there was not a needy person among them, for as many as owned lands or houses sold them and brought the proceeds of what was sold" (Acts 4:34). Insofar as the Jews anticipated the resurrection in tandem with the final restoration of Israel, these early followers of Jesus embodied the resurrection life of Jesus as the renewed people of God. Thus they were bearing witness to the possibility of living out the Sabbath and Jubilee year talked about in the Pentateuch in ways that met the needs of all the people (see Deut. 15:1–18, especially v. 4). In short, the believers' fellowship and sharing of possessions was a material realization of the redemption of Israel, a sign of the actualization of the reign of God.

The power of this testimony was not only the voluntary nature of Christian life together but also the message that it was possible to imagine a world organized otherwise. Whereas Palestine in the first century operated according to reciprocal patron-client relations—for example, between the religious elite and the masses, between landed aristocrats and their peasant workers, and between the imperial guard and their communities—for Luke the patronage relationship itself had been completely subverted since now God was the ultimate patron, Jesus was his representative, and the followers of Jesus lived in response to God's generosity instead. Rather than the sellers of property becoming beneficiaries from those who received the proceeds, it was the apostles who "distributed to each as any had need" (4:35). In turn, there is no indication the apostles claimed to be benefactors; they did not seem to own any property themselves.

The positive example here is that of Joseph, called Barnabas. A cultural foreigner (from Cyprus), Barnabas was part of the Jewish Diaspora, of the tribe of Levi. The Levitical law required living off the tithe rather than allowing for the ownership of property (see Num. 18:20; Deut. 10:9). Barnabas's conversion led him to live out the Levitical, Sabbath, and Jubilee principles: selling his field, sharing the proceeds with those in need, becoming "of one heart and soul" with other followers of Jesus, and having all things in common with them.

The negative example for the early Christian community was Ananias and his wife Sapphira. Given the voluntary nature of Christian sharing, this couple did not need to give the full amount of their sale to the apostles (5:4). Their sin was to give only part of the proceeds while pretending that was the whole, and then lying about it. Their decisions threatened the openness, selfless mutuality, and honesty of the early Christian community. When they realized their deception was found out, they "fell down . . . and died" (5:5, 10). The contrast between the life-giving practices of those like Barnabas and the community-destructive greed and dishonesty of Ananias and Sapphira was now unmistakable, and "great fear seized the whole church [ekklēsia] and all who heard of these things" (5:11). Ironically, this first reference to the *ekklēsia*[4] may also have signaled, with this shocking sequence of events, the beginning of the end of the early Christian communal experiment since, aside from discussions in Acts 6 and 11, we hear little of this type of communal sharing and generosity later on in Luke's account.

Still, the Ananias and Sapphira episode contrasts with both the candidness and the generosity of Barnabas in particular and of the wider Christian community as a whole. The early followers of Jesus bore witness with power to the resurrected Christ in part through their breaking with the patron-client structures of their time. Believers across the class and economic spectrum shared with one another without expectation of repayment because they now were a new family of brothers and sisters "of one heart and soul" (4:32) under the lordship of Christ and the apostolic leadership. They had freely received of the gracious hospitality of God and now lived out of the divine abundance against the violence, injustice, and unrighteousness of the empire and its enforcement agencies.

Is the Holy Spirit at work in similar ways today? Are there communities of faith that are signs of the coming kingdom's mutuality and friendship? These kinds of ecclesial communities by their very existence constitute a prophetic critique of the selfishness, injustice, and violence that characterize the fallen structures of this world as well as threaten to overthrow the world's way of doing business altogether. Perhaps the church's present witness to the world is muted because we are dominated by our individualism, materialism, and consumerism rather than captivated by the selflessness of Christ and of exemplars such as Barnabas. But if we fully embrace the power of the Holy Spirit instead, we will cease to compromise the gospel with our self-centeredness and actually embody the good news to the ends of the earth.

11

No "Class" Hierarchies in the Spirit!

Luke 7:18-50; 13:10-17; 18:9-17

OW CAN WE ACCOUNT for the fact that the earliest followers of Jesus "were together and had all things in common" (Acts 2:44) and "were of one heart and soul" (4:32)? How is it that these early disciples were able to break free from the class-divided and hierarchically ordered imperial structure and live with one another as equals? Perhaps this had something to do with the life and teachings of the one they followed. Perhaps he had indeed been empowered by the Spirit to restore the kingdom to Israel and did so by bringing down the mighty and lifting up the lowly (see Lk. 1:51–53) and by proclaiming release to the captives and freedom to those who were oppressed (4:18).

The Lukan passages under consideration in this chapter further highlight Jesus' leveling out the class hierarchies of his day and establishing a community of equals. We see that the poor—including the sick, demon-possessed, blind, lame, lepers, tax collectors, drunkards, and sinners at the bottom of the social hierarchy (7:21–22, 29, 34)—responded eagerly to his ministry. At the same time, it is also clear that there were others, including some Pharisees, lawyers, and religious leaders, who refused the ministries of John (and, by extension, of Jesus) and "rejected God's purpose for themselves" (7:30).

Luke's unique account of Jesus in the home of Simon the Pharisee and the ensuing interaction with the sinful woman illustrates the Spirit's calling forth a community of equals through the ministry of Jesus. Not only was it remarkable that Jesus accepted the ministry of this sinful woman to begin with, but he also clearly communicated her acceptance by God through discharging her debts (7:41–43) and forgiving her sins. (Luke 7:47 suggests that she had previously, perhaps in private, already encountered Jesus and received forgiveness, and now sought to show her gratitude to him.) The problem with Jesus' announcement of forgiveness, however, was that this had remained the prerogative of the priesthood, accomplished according to the protocols of temple sacrifices. Jesus in effect had minimized the temple ministry and, by comparing and contrasting the sinner woman with a respected Pharisee, both undermined the religious establishment and questioned the self-righteousness of Simon. (In fact, Jesus' saying to Simon, "the one to whom little is forgiven" [7:47], technically suggests that Simon has fewer sins needing absolution but in reality communicates that, of his many sins, only a few have been recognized by him as needing forgiveness!) In the end, then, Jesus' declaration that "wisdom is vindicated by all her children" (7:35) foreshadows his public justification of the sinner woman and public denunciation and condemnation of the religious hierarchy.

A similar event happens later on when Jesus is "teaching in one of the synagogues on the sabbath" (13:10). In this case, Jesus healed a woman who had been spiritually oppressed by the devil and had thereby been crippled for eighteen years. Yet the contrasting image is that of the indignant leader of the synagogue who objected that such a deed was accomplished on the Sabbath. Jesus' response was directed toward the religious leadership as a whole, which served as social and cultural gatekeepers: "You hypocrites!" (13:15). Here was a "daughter of Abraham" (13:16) who was ready to receive her Sabbath rest, over and against the religious hierarchy who seemed determined to forestall the arrival of the Day of the Lord's favor. They appeared too concerned about traditional conventions to embrace the Spirit's work of accomplishing the full restoration of Israel, especially when that included and involved the lower classes and the poor inhabitants of the land.

Jesus' later parable of the Pharisee and the tax collector (18:9–14) confirms the Spirit's leveling out the proud and lifting up the humble. The Pharisee saw himself as superior at least at three levels: morally, because he was unlike thieves, rogues, adulterers, or tax collectors; religiously, because he fasted twice a week; and economically, because he tithed faithfully. But it was the self-confessed sinful tax collector who—like Zaccheus—"went down to his home justified; . . . for all who exalt themselves will be humbled, but all who humble themselves will be exalted" (18:14).

In fact, Jesus characterizes the coming kingdom as belonging to those who are like infants and little children (18:15–17). This reflects the kind of humility that was manifest among the early believers, since none who thought themselves better than others would have been comfortable among that community of equals. Just as infants and small children require non-self-seeking hospitality, so also did the community of equals flourish through the mutuality and hospitality of people like Barnabas and other of the early followers of Jesus.

Jesus was preaching about and inviting people into a new Israel constituted by the covenant and gracious hospitality of God. On that final Sabbath rest representing the coming kingdom, debts and sins would be forgiven, people would be made whole, and the poor would be redeemed from the margins of society and restored to the center. Jesus' public ministry under the Spirit's power was frightening to the powers that be of his day because it threatened to unravel the entire hierarchical structure established by the Roman Empire. The renewal of Israel would overturn the status quo and produce a community of equals in which sinners were forgiven just like the religious leaders, in which the poor, sick, and demon-possessed were restored and reconciled with those who were well-to-do and in which despicable but sorrowful tax collectors and minimally valued infants represented the central characters of the kingdom.

I wonder if we are more like Simon the Pharisee and the synagogue leader or more like the sinner woman and the crippled woman: are we just as willing to be "lowered" from our higher statuses as we are to be "lifted up" from our lower places? I also wonder if we would have been content just to have been told, like the sinner woman, to "go in peace" (7:50), or if we would have perhaps taken the next steps of forming and then abiding within such communities of peace, forgiveness, welcome, and hospitality. We should not be happy or satisfied merely with our "individual" salvations. After all, it is the work of the Spirit, through Christ and his people, to renew Israel; to save a new and peculiar people of God; and to usher in the full kingdom of righteousness, justice, and peace (shalom). And this salvific work involves the collective dimension of all our lives, not just our solitary selves.

12
Spirit and Persecution:
The Politics of Restoration

Acts 5:12-42; 12:1-25

*J*UST AS THINGS would continue to get worse for Jesus in his dealings with the religious and political leaders of his time, so also the same would happen to his followers. Whereas they had earlier been warned and threatened by the authorities (Acts 4:21), later they are flogged (5:40) and then, in the case of James (the brother of John), executed (12:2). We may guess that hostilities increased in large part due to the felt threat that these followers of Jesus posed to the existing powers that be. People were being healed, those with unclean spirits were being delivered, the number of believers was growing from day to day and including people from the surrounding areas, and all of these uneducated and (for the most part) social misfits and outcasts were being held in increasingly high esteem (5:13–16). All of these occurrences were, of course, but an extension of the charismatic ministry of Jesus (cf. Lk. 4:18): the deeds that he did under the power of the Holy Spirit were now being accomplished by his followers, who were also empowered by the Spirit.

Just as threatening was the fact that the followers of Jesus were offering forgiveness of sins to people, as he did. Worse, they were doing so right there on the temple grounds (Acts 5:21, 25) but, like Jesus, bypassing altogether the mechanisms of the sacrificial system and the priesthood. While healers of that time would have become patrons with a large clientele, the apostles not only threatened to put such healers out of business but also refused to operate according to the accepted norms of patron-client relations. Instead, people were healed quite apart from any intentional actions of the apostles, with Peter's shadow mediating the gracious healing of God even as he walked by those who were sick (5:15).

What might have been most urgent, however, was the preaching of the apostles. In particular, the religious leaders—including the high priest and "the council and the whole body of the elders of Israel" (5:21)—were concerned that the apostles were "determined to bring this man's [Jesus'] blood on us" (5:28). To which Peter and the apostles answered in unison, reiterating the charge about "Jesus, whom you had killed by hanging him on a tree" (5:30).

The sage Gamaliel (who may have been St. Paul's teacher; 22:3) compared this mass movement to two others whose notoriety no doubt lingered in the minds of the Jewish leaders (5:36–37). Theudas rallied about four hundred, and Judas the Galilean also led a mass revolt (documented by the Jewish historian Josephus) in reaction to the tyrannical rule of Archeleus (who reigned in Judea from 4 BCE to 6 CE) and to the exorbitant taxation policies of Quirinius (of Syria). This detail may also explain why James the brother of John was executed by King Herod Agrippa (Agrippa I, who ruled in Judea from approximately 37 to 44 CE). According to the *Mishnah Sanhedrin* (9:1), beheading or execution by the sword was reserved not only for murderers, which James clearly was not, but also for apostates—those who threatened the security and stability of the region, which the leadership of the Jesus movement certainly did! In the case of Herod, it is also helpful to know that he was rather popular with the Jews (Acts 12:3), in part because he attempted to improve the status of the Jews vis-à-vis their Roman rulers. It is not difficult to imagine that he also, perhaps after prolonged discussions with the religious leaders, came to see the emerging Jesus movement as a political threat, and was not deterred by any Gamaliel-like arguments from attempting to stamp out this insurrection. He not only killed James but also had Peter thrown into prison.[5]

Amid this persecution the early followers of Jesus prayed fervently (12:5, 12) and continued to proclaim the good news of the forgiveness of sins. In response to the violence enacted on Jesus, "The God of our ancestors raised up Jesus. . . . God exalted him at his right hand as Leader and Savior, so that he might give repentance to Israel and forgiveness of sins" (5:30–31). So against the threats of the religious leaders, the apostles followed in the footsteps of their leader and Savior, offering repentance and for-giveness of sins instead. Just as Jesus had died a dishonorable and cursed death on a tree, so also the apostles "rejoiced that they were considered worthy to suffer dishonor for the sake of the name" (5:41). Rather than resisting the violence of their oppressors in like manner, the early followers of Jesus instead offered the gift of the Holy Spirit. These responses subverted the values of the empire with the values of the kingdom.

The end of Herod's life reflects the subversion of the "good news" of the *Pax Romana*. As a representative of lord Caesar, he mediated the salvific benefits of the Roman Empire in terms of distributing food to the needy, including the peoples of Tyre and Sidon (12:20); but so did the early followers of Jesus. The difference was that Herod received glory only for himself (12:22), whereas those who embraced Jesus' messiahship cared for one another as a community of equals. So the "angel of the Lord struck him down, and he was eaten by worms and died [an account confirmed in other words by Josephus]. But the word of God continued to advance and gain adherents" (12:23–24).

Through prayer and preaching, then, Luke's readers are given a vision of a nonviolent form of resistance, of a mode of ushering in the kingdom following in the footsteps of Jesus, the Spirit-empowered prophet of God. The power of the Spirit did not produce armed rebellions such as those led by Theudas and Judas the Galilean, among others (see 21:38). Instead, it inspired proclamation of a Messiah who brought about bodily healing, enacted social reconciliation between classes of people who had previously been alienated and estranged from one another, offered the forgiveness of sins, and delivered and liberated people from (social and spiritual) oppression. Those who received his invitation and were obedient in walking out his way of life were "born again" into a restored Israel, a renewed people of God, a community and fellowship of equals.

The Jews longed for such a renewal of Israel, but they did not expect it to take quite this form. The same may be said for those of us who consider ourselves followers of Jesus today. We might think about repentance, forgiveness, and the gift of the Holy Spirit in rather individualized terms. That may also explain why our witness to the resurrection of Jesus is rather muted at times without socially explosive potential. And that may also be the reason why we experience much less persecution for our faith than did the earliest followers of the Messiah.

13
The Spirit and Passion of Christ: Politics of Peace

Luke 22:31–23:56

NOT SURPRISINGLY, the same Holy Spirit who empowered the witness of the disciples (Acts 4:31; 5:32) and enabled them to persevere amid persecution even to the point of martyrdom also empowered the ministry of Jesus that led to his death. In fact, Jesus' life and passion provide a model for the disciples' emulation. Jesus even warned his followers of these things (Lk. 12:11), and he explicitly and ominously told them, "Satan has demanded to sift all of you [plural in the Greek] like wheat" (22:31). Even as he said this, Satan had already entered Judas (22:3), and the hour of "the power of darkness" (22:53) of Jesus' own trial and persecution was at hand.

Of course, the political machinery that made martyrs of the apostles was also at work in the case of Jesus. Upon his betrayal by Judas, Jesus was taken to the high priest and that morning was interrogated by the chief priests, scribes, and Jewish council. Later, he was handed over to Pilate (twice) and Herod for cross-examination, under charges of "perverting our nation, forbidding us to pay taxes to the emperor, and saying that he himself is the Messiah, a king" (23:2), and of mobilizing the crowds "by teaching throughout all Judea, from Galilee where he began even to this place" (23:5). The Jewish leaders had clearly been following each of Jesus' steps since he had begun his journey through Galilee to Jerusalem some time back (9:51) and had observed how enthralled the people were by his message and deeds. It was probably these same crowds from Galilee and Judea who also were drawn to Jerusalem later on during the apostolic revival (Acts 5:16).

Of course, the apostles were guilty of the charges against them—of inspiring the people, preaching about Jesus, and offering the forgiveness of sins—although they did so not directly intending to overturn the religious and political status quo. By contrast, Jesus was plainly not guilty of the charges against him. Yet these charges were brought because the religious leaders sensed that he was about overturning the status quo even if they could not quite figure out how he intended to do so. Thus, in response to their trumped up accusations of treason and sedition, Luke is careful to tell us that Jesus did not forbid paying taxes to Caesar (Lk. 20:25), and while he did stir up the people, he was not seeking to bring about an armed rebellion as they feared. So while Jesus even affirmed being the messianic Son of God and king of the Jews—thus leading to the inscription "This is the King of the Jews" on the cross (23:38)—his innocence is recognized and repeatedly declared across the various phases of his "trial": by Pilate (thrice), Herod Antipas, one of the criminals on the cross, the centurion at the foot of the cross, and, implicitly, Joseph of Arimathea, who did not agree with the council's prosecution of Jesus. Not surprisingly, Jesus is also proclaimed as the "Righteous One" by the apostles later on (Acts 3:14).

Ironically, while Gamaliel compared the apostles to the insurrectionists Theudas and Judas the Galilean, Jesus was executed in the place of Barabbas, "who had been put in prison for an insurrection that had taken place in the city, and for murder" (Lk. 23:19, 25). Against the violence of Barabbas and other aspiring Messiahs, however, Jesus advocated a way of peace (19:42; cf. 1:79; 2:14). Yes, this was a time of crisis, as symbolized by the sword that

Jesus called attention to (22:36). But while the disciples thought this meant the time had come to free Israel from imperial rule, they had missed his point. In response to their producing two swords for the task they believed at hand, Jesus exclaims in exasperation, "It is enough!" (22:38); and to the violent response against Judas and the crowd, he commands, "No more of this!" (22:51), and promotes healing and peace instead. Even when he is mocked, scoffed at, and beaten (22:63–65; 23:11, 35–36, 39), Jesus refuses to retaliate.

After Pentecost, the disciples clearly had learned to emulate the nonviolent way of Jesus. While they could not stay awake when he prepared himself through prayer to confront the opposition, they later repeatedly looked not to the sword but to prayer and the power of the Spirit (Acts 4:24–30; 12:5). Jesus' determination to be obedient to the Father, even to the point of death on the cross, provided a model for the disciples' own nonviolent resistance. Thus the disciples' repeated offering of the forgiveness of sins in their preaching was a reflection of Jesus' response, both in his life and at his death: "Father, forgive them; for they do not know what they are doing" (Lk. 23:34).

We have already seen that Jesus, and John before him, offered the forgiveness of sins on behalf of the Father long before his death (3:3; 5:20; 7:47–48). It should be noted that, unlike the other New Testament writers, Luke has no concept of Jesus' death as a substitution or satisfaction for sins. Rather, Jesus clearly expected to die as an innocent man in a political confrontation with the authorities— and he did!—but he also expected God to vindicate his life's mission (to renew and redeem Israel) and messiahship through a resurrection from the dead (9:22; 18:33; 22:69). The apostles understood the death, resurrection, *and* exaltation of Jesus as being central to the availability of forgiveness of sins. God's plan for the renewal of Israel thus appeared to involve Jesus' demonstration of a way of peace; his execution despite his innocence; God's vindicating Jesus as Messiah through the resurrection; and the consequent offer of peace, reconciliation, and abundant life—the ultimate Sabbath rest, Jubilee year, and Day of the Lord's favor—through the forgiveness of sins committed against God and his innocent Messiah.

Jesus had come, full of the Spirit's power, to restore and renew Israel and to establish the kingdom of God. In his passion and death, it seemed to his disciples that his plan was thwarted. But there may have been some, including Joseph of Arimathea, who intuited otherwise. Joseph did not go along with his fellow council members apparently because, unlike them, he "was waiting expectantly for the kingdom of God" (23:51; like Simeon and Anna before him) and recognized, however faintly, that Jesus' life, ministry, and even death pointed to its dawning in their midst. The way forward for Israel was not through taking up the sword but through embodying the peace, righteousness, and justice displayed in the life of the Messiah. All of this called not for passivity in the face of opposition but for faithful reliance on God. After Pentecost, the disciples finally seemed to have got it!

Those of us today who have been and are recipients of the gift of the Holy Spirit ought then to live out the values and manifest the practices of the kingdom that Jesus came to establish. We should be like the early disciples, who followed in the path of Jesus, lived out his vision, and carried his burden—just as Simeon of Cyrene did (23:26). We should be just as guilty today as was Jesus and his earliest followers of threatening to overturn the status quo, of freely forgiving the sins of others, and of anticipating a new world order of shalom amid a world of violence. We should pray not to ignore the work of the Holy Spirit or be too caught up with the kingdoms of this world when we ought to be hastening the kingdom of God.

14

Multiculturalism, Globalization, and the Spirit

Acts 6:1-7; 11:19-30

*J*ESUS' MISSION of restoring Israel and establishing the kingdom birthed an alternative form of life. This assembly of God (*ekklēsia*) that had been filled with the Holy Spirit on the Day of Pentecost was initially constituted by Diaspora Jews and proselytes from around the known (Mediterranean) world and continued to add to its numbers local inhabitants from around the Judean countryside. Yet this community of equals, despite their generous practices of sharing that had, for a time, resulted in the needs of each being met, were about to confront their first major intercultural and economic challenges.

Acts 6 tells us that the apostles' attempts to serve the multitudes had reached a breaking point. Ironically, this was set off by their realization that there were some in the community—Hellenists, Luke calls them, referring in all probability to Greek-speaking Diaspora Jews (and proselytes)—who were being treated as less than equals because of apostolic neglect. Things had changed since the early days of the movement, when the disciples broke bread with one another in their homes. The tremendous growth of the Jesus movement had strained the limited resources of the community, and the large numbers involved led naturally to communal pockets that developed along class, cultural, ethnic, and linguistic lines.

The most vulnerable groups in the community, the widows, had thus gathered into two distinct congregations: Greek-speaking, probably representing those who had returned to Palestine from the Diaspora after their husbands had deceased, and Hebrew-speaking, consisting of locals. The problem seems to have been that the Hellenistic widows "were being neglected in the daily distribution of food" (Acts 6:1). But the Greek text actually says only that they were neglected in the daily *diakonia*, better translated simply as "services" or "distribution"; it is only the response of the Twelve—who distinguished between the "word of God" and "waiting tables" (6:2)—that leads to the translation of *diakonia* as "distribution of food." Yet this does not seem quite right since, at the sociocultural level, the preparation, distribution, and serving of food would have been the responsibility of women. Further, the seven men who are appointed to oversee this matter are never said to have taken up the work of food distribution; instead, with two of them (Stephen and Philip; Acts 6:8–8:8), we are told of their preaching the word of God with power.

It appears that Acts 6 reflects the challenges to maintaining a community of equals that confront any multicultural, multiethnic, and multilinguistic community. Human propensity leads us to gather with others of similar background and experiences; there is nothing inherently wrong with this. However, this Palestinian movement was under local (i.e., Aramaic-speaking) leadership, and this in turn led, probably inadvertently, to the marginalization of the Hellenistic widows—"resident aliens" who were without family or social support—from active participation in the daily service-provision and activities of the community. The apostolic response was to appoint and empower Greek-speaking leaders (the names of the seven are all Hellenistic) to ensure that such exclusionary and unjust behaviors and practices would be corrected and that these widows would be adequately cared for. One of these Spirit-filled leaders was Nicolaus, "a proselyte of Antioch" (Acts 6:5).

Nicolaus and his family may have visited Jerusalem on the Day of Pentecost with other Diaspora Jews from Antioch and the surrounding region. They had joined the apostolic community and his leadership abilities were recognized and confirmed. In all probability, these Antiochene Jews and proselytes had other family members who remained in Antioch. It is probable that the various Greek- and Hebrew-speaking Jewish communities, connected by common religious beliefs, practices, and aspirations, found common cause with the apostolic vision even if they spoke different languages. Still, it was predictable that the persecution of the messianic community in Jerusalem led to a scattering of the faithful and that many of these converts simply returned to their homes (or second homes, in the case of Diaspora Jews) and brought the good news with them.

This is exactly how the gospel arrived in Antioch, through Nicolaus and other Antiochenes. This was an important development for the early messianic community since Antioch was widely recognized in the first century as the third-greatest city in the Roman Empire (besides Rome and Alexandria), with a population of about half a million inhabitants. It is here that these messianic believers first came to be known as *christianos*, or followers of the anointed one, the Messiah (11:26), even if this name did not take root as a Christian self-understanding until the second century. (The word *christianos* only occurs twice elsewhere in the New Testament: in Acts 26:28, on the lips of Agrippa II, who asks Paul, "Are you so quickly persuading me to become a Christian?" and in 1 Peter 4:16, which says, "Yet if any of you suffers as a Christian, do not consider it a disgrace, but glorify God because you bear this name.")

Probably sometime during the second decade of the existence of this messianic community, a worldwide (the original Greek is *oikoumenēn*) famine set in. At least this is what Agabus, a prophet, predicted (11:27–28). Luke's aside, that this happened "during the reign of Claudius" (which dated from 41–54), is confirmed by the references in extrabiblical texts to a rather severe drought that devastated the grain crops of Egypt during the years 45–47. In effect, while the drought may have been local to Egypt, it had "global" implications, not only for those regions of the known (imperial) world that were dependent on the Egyptian grain export (as were the inhabitants of Palestine) but also for those diasporic communities who were connected to those hit hardest by the scarcity of grain and the resulting inflation of grain prices (as were Diaspora Jews in relationship to family "back home").

The Antiochene Christians responded to this need by sending relief to their Judean brothers and sisters through Barnabas and Saul, and this seems to be confirmed by Saul (Paul) himself (see Gal. 2:1–10, esp. v. 10). Whereas the gospel of Jesus the Messiah had come out of the "mother" church in Judea, the ministries of "daughter" churches, such as the one at Antioch, were now flowing back home. These developments suggest that Christian mission resists any kind of hierarchical, patriarchal, or "colonial" mentality, and emphasizes a mutuality and reciprocity between "sending" and "receiving" churches instead.

In one sense, little has changed in two thousand years except that the "empire" of market capitalism has replaced the Roman Empire of the first century. What remains now, as then, are the marginalization of cultural and linguistic "outsiders" in any local situation, the ever-present needs of the poor worldwide (both within and outside Christian communities), shifting migrant and even refugee communities (perhaps fleeing from persecution of some sort or other), and the instabilities endured by a volatile political economy (with global implications commensurate with the global economy and globalization processes, as our current dependence on oil continually reminds us). Yet we can learn a very important lesson from the early messianic believers that remains applicable for our time: that effective leadership and ministry must represent and respect the perspectives and languages of the people who need to be served. This is no more than an extension of the Pentecost principle wherein the gospel was announced to the crowd in their own languages by the power of the Holy Spirit. The apostolic leaders recognized the importance of this principle by involving Greek-speaking Hellenists on their "leadership team," and "the word of God continued to spread" (Acts 6:7).

This appears to have carried over into the initial ministry to Antioch, where a "great number became believers and turned to the Lord" (11:21). The ministries of Barnabas and Saul both added to the success of the establishment of the church at Antioch (11:24–26). In the final analysis, the Pentecost principle allowed the apostolic leaders to affirm the initiative, agency, and distinctive ministries of the Antiochene church on its own terms, and it seemed good to the Holy Spirit that this in turn produced a "reverse mission" of blessing from Antioch back to the churches in Judea. This is precisely what the Holy Spirit continues to do today amid a world marked by inequalities between the West and the rest, and by poverty especially in the developing nations of the Global South. Africans and Asians, who once were recipients of missionaries from the Western world, are now coming as missionaries to Europe and North America, bringing the gospel with them to secularized lands. The Spirit remains at work in multicultural sites, reconciling but yet preserving the many tongues and languages of people.

15

Poverty and Possessions: Spirit-Filled Life and the Global Economy

Luke 12:13-34; 16:10-31; 18:18-30; 20:45-21:4

THE EARLIEST FOLLOWERS OF JESUS who repented and received the Holy Spirit lived as a community of equals who had all things in common. Those who were more well off sold what they had and shared the proceeds so that there were none who had need. As the church expanded from Jerusalem into Judea and Samaria and beyond, congregations separated by region, geography, language, culture, and ethnicity stood in solidarity with one another, providing relief for one another as needed. A new people of God was emerging that transcended the common divisions of the first century, brothers and sisters who acknowledged the same Father as did Jesus, as inspired by the Holy Spirit. They represented a countercultural way of life, opting out of the accepted political, economic, and social conventions established by the Roman Empire.

In many ways, however, these earliest believers had simply embraced the life and teachings of their Messiah, as handed down through the apostles. As we shall see in Luke—and I urge the reader to have the New Testament close at hand—Jesus' views about wealth, possessions, and poverty were clearly adopted in the early messianic communities. Most importantly, on two separate occasions, Jesus encouraged his followers to sell what they had and give alms to the poor (Lk. 12:33; 18:22). Unlike others who hoarded up for themselves, the disciples are encouraged to strive after the kingdom instead (12:30–31). Indeed, from a human point of view, the more affluent found this to be a hard teaching, and the disciples agreed that on these terms, none could be saved (18:23–26). However, Jesus insisted that "what is impossible for mortals is possible for God" (18:27), and upon receipt of the Holy Spirit, ordinary believers like Barnabas led the way in demonstrating the possibility of living out the abundant generosity and hospitality of God.

The problem, of course, was that most human beings are, like the Pharisees Luke indicted, "lovers of money" (16:14). Ananias and Sapphira failed to heed Jesus' warnings about being greedy; about storing up earthly rather than heavenly treasures; about worrying over the basic necessities of life; and about trying to serve God and mammon. Of course, most of Jesus' listeners assumed that wealth, riches, and possessions were a sign of divine blessing following upon their obedience to the covenant (cf. Deut. 28:1–14). However, Jesus was reminding them that the covenant promises of God were made with an undeserving people who were generally the poor, the oppressed, and the marginalized. In fact, these were the ones to whom the good news of the kingdom was being proclaimed (Lk. 4:18; 7:22), and it was precisely the poor, the sick, and the demon-possessed (Acts 5:16) who were responding to the proclamation of the kingdom.

That the new people of God included these marginalized folk led by uneducated men (4:13) was hinted at early in Luke's Gospel. Mary (in the Magnificat) had foretold the reversals of the kingdom: the uplifting of the lowly, the humble, and the poor, and the lowering of the powerful, the proud, and the rich (Lk. 1:51–53). Jesus' parables and teachings reaffirm this central feature of the kingdom. The rich are called fools because their calculations for earthly success are mistaken, while disciples who trust God to provide for their daily needs are those who are full of the Holy Spirit. The unnamed rich man who receives a decent burial (thinking himself a true child of Abraham) actually finds himself tormented in Hades, while a named (Lazarus), poor (homeless), unclean (with sores), impure (contaminated by licking dogs), and probably crippled (who is "thrown down" at the rich man's gate; 16:20) man who is not said to have received a proper burial finds himself in the bosom of Abraham. Even the scribes who are "greeted with respect in the marketplaces, and . . . have the best seats in the synagogues and places of honour at banquets" actually oppress the very widows they are supposed to care for and are thereby condemned (20:46–47), while the poor widow herself is affirmed as one who is living out the values of the kingdom (21:2–4). These reversals in the teachings of Jesus are exemplified in the messianic community that lived not according to the ways of the world but according to the power of the Holy Spirit.

The rich and affluent are unfortunately too self-centered. They are caught up in the economy of greed and profit, which occurs usually at the expense of the masses in the underclasses. Those who have caught a vision of the kingdom, however, are those who are able to see others beyond themselves. They are not self-consumed but have learned the spirit of the great commandments, which is to love God and neighbor fully. Note that, in response to the rich man's question about how to attain eternal life, Jesus identified the five commandments that address how we treat others (18:20). In the end, the love of God and the pursuit of the kingdom will result in a love for neighbor that reconstitutes ourselves and our neighbors as a new family and people of God (18:29–30; cf. 8:19–21).

The outpouring of the Spirit on all flesh was the next step in God's plan to restore and renew Israel—precisely through the establishment of an expanded family of brothers and sisters who would love one another as the Father loved the Son and the Son the Father. Those who were of means provided for others, expecting nothing in return. The mutuality and sharing reconciled the rich and the poor and brought together those who had been divided by language, culture, ethnicity, and class. These who were called Christians—followers of the Messiah—served one another and ate together without regard to the protocols of the world. Such was the imitation of the life of Jesus, the works of the Holy Spirit, the way of the kingdom.

PART FOUR

Leaving Judea?
A Theological Excursus

16

A Hellenistic Account of Israel's Story: The Work of the Spirit and the "Ends of the Earth"

Acts 6:8–8:1

ESUS' TEACHINGS about possessions, poverty, and wealth illuminate the economic dimension of God's plan to restore and redeem Israel. But Luke's account of Stephen's ministry and martyrdom shows that there are other related aspects of the redemption of Israel. In fact, the circumstances surrounding Stephen's life and death reconnect us with the major plotline of Acts: the expansion of the gospel from Jerusalem and Judea to Samaria and the ends of the earth (Acts 1:8). From a perspective twenty centuries later, it is sometimes difficult for contemporary readers to understand that carrying and translating the gospel from a predominantly Judean-based movement to a Gentile audience was for a long time seriously contested. A careful reconsideration of the Stephen story and what happened in its aftermath is crucially important for understanding how this transition was resisted and then achieved. As will be clear, the God of Israel has always had in mind both the underside of history and the ends of the earth rather than just being focused only on a "deserving" people or on the land promised to her ancestors.

I suggest it is not coincidental that Stephen's telling of Israel's history has a more "universal" flavor to it. After all, we know that Stephen was a Hellenistic Jew, perhaps one who had returned from the Diaspora to take up residence among the messianic community in Jerusalem and experienced firsthand the possibility of local flourishing amid imperial developments across the Greek-speaking world. His apology, in response to fellow Hellenistic Jews from around the Mediterranean (6:9), begins by calling attention to the origins of Israel's "founding father," Abraham, a lifelong sojourner from Mesopotamia, Haran, and the land of the Chaldeans (7:2, 4). He himself never received the land promised to him, and is even buried in Shechem (7:16) on the Judean-Samarian border (perhaps anticipating the gospel's arrival in Samaria in Acts 8).

Later, the patriarchs of Israel (Joseph, his brothers, and their descendents) were formatively shaped as "resident aliens" (7:6) for over four hundred years in the land of Egypt. Moses himself was "instructed in all the wisdom of the Egyptians" (7:22), even as he later spent forty years as a refugee in Midian (7:23, 29–30), what is today known as the Sinai Peninsula. It is Moses, of course, whom God used to lead Israel out of their Egyptian captivity back to the land of Canaan (promised to Abraham), although the people resisted his leadership in various ways (7:27–28, 39–40). In all of this, we see that God called out for himself a people who were not originally a people. Instead, anticipating the outpouring of the Spirit on all flesh at Pentecost (2:17), Israel had been formed out of the languages, cultures, and nations of what we now call the ancient Near East.

What should not be overlooked in Stephen's retelling of this story is the role of the Holy Spirit. Here I am referring not only to the fact that Stephen was a man full of the Holy Spirit (6:3, 5) and that his rendition was inspired by the Holy Spirit (7:55); but Stephen also clearly declared that, in one sense, the entire history of Israel involved the Jewish people's opposition to the work of the Spirit (7:51). While the Spirit of God had called a peculiar people out of the ancient Near Eastern world, they had continuously resisted that calling, disobeyed God, and even exchanged the worship of God for idols. The result, of course, was the Babylonian exile (7:43), which over the course of the next few centuries shaped the diasporic existence of the Jews under imperial Rome.

Not surprisingly, Hellenistic Jews in the Diaspora often found their way back to Judea, motivated by the promises of God made to Abraham. In fact, Stephen's opponents were themselves Jewish "Freedmen" (6:9), former slaves who served at various centers throughout the Roman Empire but upon release had returned to Judea. They also were no doubt longing for the redemption of Israel from imperial rule, being zealous defenders of the law of Moses, the land of Israel, and the temple of Yahweh, understood as the dwelling place of God himself (7:46). In fact, Stephen was charged precisely with speaking against these central Jewish symbols (6:11, 13–14).

Like the elders, scribes, high priests, and religious council, the Sanhedrin (6:12; 7:1), the Hellenistic freedmen also felt threatened by the nascent but growing messianic community. Not only was there now an alternative for Hellenistic widows among the followers of Jesus (6:1–6), but there was also the increasing realization that the practices of these believers threatened to undermine the role of the temple in the religious and cultural life of Israel. If Jesus and his disciples were right, there was no more need for sacrifices for sins (God seemingly has chosen to dispense forgiveness in Jesus' name), no need for a priesthood (the Twelve were not of the tribe of Levi), and perhaps no need for the temple at all. (We shall see in the next chapter that Jesus did foretell the destruction of the temple.)

The twelve apostles may still also have been expecting some kind of redemption of Israel and the temple from Roman rule.

(Until now we have heard only that the apostles continued to meet daily in the temple precincts.) But it is the Hellenistic and cosmopolitan Stephen who somehow came to the insight that the God of Israel was also in a sense the God of all nations—of Mesopotamians, Chaldeans, Egyptians, Midianites, and so on—and that God's "dwelling place" was not limited to a specific region or locale (whether Judea, Jerusalem, or even the temple). Instead, all of heaven and earth belonged to the Lord (7:49). If so, then the redemption and renewal of Israel suggested also the salvation of all people, not just the Jews. And in that case, the children of those who had persecuted the prophets and murdered Jesus were being overly parochial and wrongly exclusivistic.

These zealous Jews were enraged (7:54) by what they heard, just as the same council of religious leaders had been before, to the point of wishing to kill the apostles (5:33). While previously there had been a Gamaliel to hold them back, in this case there was only another leading Hellenistic Jew, a Cilician himself (21:39; 22:3; 23:34) who no doubt resonated with the convictions of his fellow Cilician freedmen (6:9) and approved of their defending the old faith. Stephen's vision of seeing "the heavens opened and the Son of Man standing at the right hand of God" (7:56) probably triggered recollections of Jesus' own claim to that effect (Lk. 22:69) and resulted in his execution.

From here on out, the Good News would expand from Judea (among local, diasporic, and Hellenistic Jews and proselytes to Judaism) to Samaria, to the Gentiles, and to Rome itself. But before we look at the unfolding of the work of the Spirit to the ends of the earth, we must pause to examine in more detail Jesus' own understanding of the place of Israel, Jerusalem, and the temple in the salvific plan of God.

17

Judgment on Jerusalem: The Spirit and the Redemption of Israel

Luke 13:1-5, 31-35; 19:41-44; 20:9-19; 21:5-38

TEPHEN WAS STONED BY HELLENISTIC JEWISH FREEDMEN and members of the Sanhedrin. While the charges against Stephen were concocted by his opponents, their claims that he spoke against Moses, the law, and temple were at least partially grounded in Jesus' own words. Jesus himself said of the temple, "The days will come when not one stone will be left upon another; all will be thrown down" (Lk. 21:6). It appears that part of Stephen's witness (Acts 6:9–10) before his fateful apology had to do with an elaboration of this prophecy of Jesus; certainly his last words did, which included the declaration that "the Most High does not dwell in houses made by human hands" (7:48), least of all in the temple, which, while ordered to be rebuilt by Herod the Great in 20/19 BCE, was still under reconstruction (cf. Jn. 2:20) in Jesus' lifetime. So even if Stephen never did reject the Mosaic law—in fact, he accuses his hearers of not listening to Moses and the prophets— his words as well as Jesus' were open to misunderstanding by those already overzealous for the traditions of the ancestors.

Yet it's important to locate Jesus' prediction about the temple against the background of his warnings regarding the destruction of Jerusalem as a whole. As the city was the symbol of national power, Jesus set his face to travel to Jerusalem (Lk. 9:51). But its inhabitants were resistant, recognizing neither "the things that make for peace" nor "the time of [their] visitation from God"; thus Jesus foretold: "The days will come upon you, when your enemies will set up ramparts around you and surround you, and hem you in on every side. They will crush you to the ground, you and your children within you, and they will not leave within you one stone upon another" (19:42–44). Thus will come a time of wars and insurrections (21:9) when Jerusalem will be surrounded by armies (21:20) and "will be trampled on by the Gentiles" (21:24; cf. 23:28–31). This devastation actually did occur about forty years later, at the hands of the Romans in the war of 66–70 CE, with the temple being demolished in the process.

Jesus' pronouncements regarding Jerusalem and the temple are complicated by a number of factors. While there is some scholarly consensus that the Gospel was written sometime after 70 CE, there is no satisfactory explanation as to why Luke does not clearly emphasize the fulfillment of these words. Then there are at least three major schools of thought about how to understand Jesus' prophecies: (1) that they were literally fulfilled in the Jewish-Roman war; (2) that they admit of multiple fulfillments since the time of Jesus, and perhaps into the future; and (3) that while some parts of the prophecy were fulfilled by 70 CE, ultimate fulfillment of much of what was said remains ahead even of us today. The ambiguity regarding his statement that "this generation will not pass away until all things have taken place" (21:32) is indicative of the difficulties: does "this generation" refer to that of Jesus' hearers (ca. 30 CE), to that which experienced the wrath of Rome (66–70 CE), or to that which sees the "Son of Man coming in a cloud" (21:27)? I see no reason to deny that there is some truth in each school of thought, even as I am wary about making specific correlations between Jesus' words and contemporary world events.

More important, I think, is that Jesus clearly linked his fate with that of Jerusalem. He implored its inhabitants to repent of their ways (13:3, 5), of their idolatry, of their disobedience to the covenant of God, of their personal and social sins, and of their nationalism and violence. He also discerned that his message of peace (19:42), forgiveness, and justice would be rejected by scribes and chief priests (20:19) and that the ensuing confrontation with the Jewish leaders (20:14–15) would result in his death in Jerusalem (13:32–33). But worse was his anticipation that this rejection and its concomitant violence would only perpetuate the nationalist aspirations of the Jewish people and would precipitate a sequence of events culminating in a national conflagration. This was exactly what happened by 70 CE. The violence wielded by the Jewish leaders to maintain the status quo—in the case of Jesus first and then later against Stephen and James—was but a reflection of the underlying unrest, ferment, and turmoil that permeated the nation. Insurrection after insurrection finally brought about the violent military response of Rome.

Let us step back for a moment to recapitulate the big picture of what the Holy Spirit had sought to do through the lives of Jesus and his followers. Jesus had come to restore Israel and establish the kingdom of God by the power of the Spirit. Israel (along with the disciples, at least at first) had assumed that such redemption meant the overthrowing of Roman rule and the reestablishment of the nation and its temple under Jewish auspices. Any such political revolution would have been at odds with the values of the kingdom. Instead, Jesus invited repentance from the ways of the world and freely offered the forgiveness of sins. He understood his own life to be a fulfillment of the law and a replacement of the temple sacrifices. Acceptance of his messianic leadership would lead to the formation of a new Israel, a new people of God who would live not according to the politics, economics, or military conventions of this world but according to that of the kingdom.

Even after Jesus was killed for his nonviolent but revolutionary activities, the Spirit of God who empowered his message to the poor came upon his disciples and established just that new community of equals and of common goods. The apostles, including Hellenistic Jews like Stephen and his fellow deacons, continued to preach repentance, forgiveness, healing, and salvation in Jesus' name; to lift up Jesus' life as fulfilling the law; and to view the followers of the Messiah as being the new site of the presence of God (instead of the temple). They were thus persecuted by the Jewish leaders because their message and way of life threatened the status quo. Throughout history and around the world today, those who by the power of the Spirit have embodied the teachings of Jesus and lived out the revolutionary good news of the kingdom have been opposed for bucking the systems of this age.

While Jesus had admonished the religious leaders that their non-repentance would result in the leadership of Israel being given over to others (20:16), he had also warned the Jewish people that their unrepentant hearts would bring about not only the destruction of Jerusalem but also the opportunity for the Gentiles to participate in the coming kingdom (13:29). Actually, as we see in Stephen's speech, Israel herself was constituted by those out of many tribes, tongues, and nations, even while the new people of God was similarly established on the Day of Pentecost from out of a plurality of languages and cultures. Christians today, who are predominantly Gentile, do not think too much about this, but in Stephen's time, it was a truly scandalous proposal. Still, even the most progressive of messianic followers then might hardly have imagined the Spirit's outpouring on all flesh extended even to the despised Samaritans.

PART FIVE

*The Spirit Moves into Samaria and on
the Highways of Ancient Palestine*

18
Samaria: The Spirit Meets the "Religious Other"

Acts 8:1-25; cf. Luke 9:51-56; 10:25-37; 17:11-19

*W*E SHOULD NOT UNDERESTIMATE the extent to which the hostilities between Jews and Samaritans led the former to exclude the latter from being considered as belonging to the people of God and from participating in the redemption and renewal of Israel. The origins of the Samaritans—during the eighth century BCE, when Samaria was taken over by the Assyrians (2 Kgs. 17:24–41)—were seen by the Jews to have involved a syncretism with foreign beliefs and practices. It did not help that during the second-century-BCE persecution of the Jews by the Romans, the Samaritans denied any affiliation with the Jews and even for a time permitted their temple on Mount Gerizim (in Samaria) to be known as the temple of Zeus Hellenios.

By the time of Jesus, Jews and Samaritans had an ambiguous relationship. Samaritans accepted the Torah (the first five books of Moses), but nothing else in the Hebrew canon; they rejected the significance of Jerusalem, insisting on true worship as taking place on Mount Gerizim instead (Jn. 4:20); and yes, they awaited a Messiah (Jn. 4:25), but one in the tradition of Moses (Deut. 18:15–18). The result was that Samaritans were viewed by Jews at best as being a corrupted and apostate form of true Judaism (cf. Jn. 4:9)—like some contemporary Christians would view sectarian and cultic groups—or at worst as being a false religion altogether. The feelings were mutual: Samaritans were antagonistic toward Jerusalem and all that it stood for (see Lk. 9:52–53); and Jews sometimes understood the Samaritans as being demon-possessed (see Jn. 8:48).

It may be no coincidence, then, that it was Philip, a Hellenistic Jew, who first took the gospel to the Samaritans rather than the apostles, who, despite the persecution, remained in Jerusalem (Acts 8:1). While the apostles were still very much focused on a redemption of Israel in an exclusive sense, Philip may have just followed Stephen's Hellenistic-Jewish view that the true worship of God is not limited to any temple or sacred place (7:48–50) and concluded that the presence of God was just as available to the Samaritans, who were gathered around another holy site. So whereas the Samaritans had previously rejected Jesus, they now received Philip, who simply extended under the power of the Spirit the ministry of Jesus to the poor, sick, and oppressed (8:6–12).

We are not told that Philip rejected any of the Samaritan beliefs and practices in his interaction with the inhabitants of Samaria. What was definitively rejected, especially by the apostles Peter and John who came to provide backup support to Philip, was the greed, desire for authority, and sinful intents of Simon the magician, who sought to "obtain God's gift with money!" (Acts 8:20). The generosity of God, as we have seen, does not operate according to the world's economy of exchange and payment; rather, God freely gives the Spirit, although in the case of the Samaritans, through the laying on of the apostles' hands. The result, Luke tells us, is that "the church throughout Judea, Galilee, and Samaria had peace and was built up. Living in the fear of the Lord and in the comfort of the Holy Spirit, it increased in numbers" (9:31).

Thus was the mission to Samaria a middle step between the gospel's procession from Judea and its surroundings to the ends of the world, and this was already signaled in the Gospel narrative. Whereas in Matthew's Gospel Jesus prohibited the Twelve from evangelizing the Samaritans (Matt. 10:5), this embargo is not found in Luke's account. Instead, Jesus "sent messengers ahead of him . . . [and] they entered a village of the Samaritans to make ready for him" (Lk. 9:52).

Later on his way to Jerusalem, as he was leaving Samaria on the other side of the region (17:11), he encountered and healed ten lepers, one of whom was a Samaritan. While Jesus clearly recognized this Samaritan as a "foreigner" (17:18)—*allomenos*, meaning one who was not a son of Abraham, as Jews understood themselves—yet he also just as clearly affirmed, "Get up and go on your way; your faith has made you well" (17:19). So although the other nine (Jewish) lepers were physically cured and socially rehabilitated (cleansing from leprosy allowed one to be reintegrated into the community), only this one Samaritan was declared to have been saved and made fully whole. In at least this sense, the Samaritan showed himself to be more discerning about Jesus' mission and identity than his fellow Jewish compatriots.

While the possibility of the salvation of Samaritans would have shocked many Jews, Jesus' own teachings should have prepared them to question their religious assumptions and self-assuredness. Note that Jesus told the famous parable of the good Samaritan (10:29–37) in response to the Jewish lawyer's attempt to justify himself by asking, "Who is my neighbor?" That itself was motivated by his original question about how to inherit eternal life and Jesus' well-known response that it required loving God fully and loving our neighbors as ourselves (10:25–28).

This whole episode is just as suggestive today for Christians thinking about religious pluralism as it was two thousand years ago for Jews thinking about Samaritans, religious others, and those whom they thought were demon-possessed. It suggests (1) that there may be those in other "faiths," like this Samaritan, who do love God and their neighbor more than those of us who think we have access to God's saving grace and that these others therefore may be closer to eternal life than we are; (2) that we might actually be able to learn something important from those in other faiths whom we have previously thought were without the truth, just as this Jewish lawyer was being taught by the good Samaritan; and (3) that those in other faiths may actually be instruments used by God for our own salvation (health and healing) just as the man who fell among robbers received his salvation from his Samaritan neighbor. Jesus' parable about the good Samaritan thus not only shattered first-century Jewish presumptions about themselves and Samaritans but also anticipated that the gospel would eventually proceed into Samaria and that they would be included among the new people of God.

Were not these overturning of presumptions in line with the radical new world that the Spirit of God would bring about through Jesus and those who followed in his steps? Even if the apostles themselves did not lead the way into Samaria, they followed Philip, who was empowered by the Holy Spirit to conduct exorcisms, heal the sick, and preach the good news of the kingdom of the Messiah. Then God confirmed this ministry by not withholding his very self, the Holy Spirit, even from those despised Samaritans!

19

The Spirit Meets the Ethiopian Eunuch: Redeeming Disability

Acts 8:26-40; cf. Luke 14:1-24

IF THE INCLUSION OF THE DESPISED SAMARITANS in the coming kingdom was a stretch for many Jews of the first century, so also was the inclusion of the Ethiopian eunuch, although for other reasons. This man, known to us as the Ethiopian eunuch, had three strikes against him: (1) he was from the outskirts of the empire, thought then to be situated at the southern edge of human civilization; (2) he was probably of darker skin, as were those from Cush, Nubia, and Ethiopia (south of Egypt), and thus viewed by some as racially suspect or marginal; and (3) he was a eunuch, therefore probably castrated, and as such considered effeminate and not a fully able-bodied male. In some ways, strikes one and two were not as damaging, especially given some of the prophecies regarding the inclusion of Cushites and Ethiopians eventually in the redemption and restoration of Israel (Ps. 68:31; Isa. 45:14; Zeph. 3:9–10), and the inclusive outpouring of the Spirit on all flesh on the Day of Pentecost.

Being a eunuch may have been more problematic for first-century Jews, especially since the law excluded eunuchs and those with crushed testicles from participating in the liturgical cult and worship of ancient Israel (Deut. 23:1). Of course, castrated males were not being singled out; rather, they were categorized among those with physical, sensorial, and functional disabilities: the blind, lame, mutilated, hunchbacked, dwarfed, and so on (Lev. 21:17–23). The Torah then later also clearly connected these "disabilities" with divine punishment for sin and disobedience (Deut. 28:15–68). The result was so that even though in one case Jesus denied the link between the man born blind and the sins of himself or his parents (Jn. 9:2–3), his response in another case to the paralytic—"Do not sin any more, so that nothing worse happens to you" (Jn. 5:14)—as well as his linking sickness, blindness, deafness, and dumbness with evil spirits and healing these through exorcisms fit first-century Jewish assumptions about disability.

Yet Luke's inclusive vision of the redemption of Israel and the kingdom of God is revealed even in this case of people long marginalized because of their various disabilities. Just as Jesus had accepted the socially despised and short-statured Zaccheus (see our discussion above in chapter 5), so also here Philip accepts the racially questionable and physically impaired eunuch. Yes, in many other cases, Jesus and the apostles healed the sick and "disabled" by the power of the Spirit. However, in these two cases, Jesus pronounced the arrival of salvation to Zaccheus's household (Lk. 19:9) and Philip baptized the eunuch (Acts 8:38) without any reversal of their physical conditions.

The acceptance of the eunuch began to fulfill the promise of Yahweh to include eunuchs in the final redemption of Israel (Isa. 56:3–5). Perhaps not coincidentally, the eunuch was reading about this final restoration when Philip came alongside his chariot. As one without the prospect of having children, the eunuch perhaps wondered about the fate and legacy of this figure he was reading about who also died without any descendents (Acts 8:32–33). Ethiopian tradition traces the origins of the church in that region to this eunuch's testimony. With his conversion, then, Luke not only anticipates the taking of the gospel to the ends of the known world but also clearly affirms that the diversity of tongues, cultures, and races in the coming kingdom includes the differences represented by human bodies.

Jesus' own teachings foreshadowed the inclusion of people like the eunuch. In Luke 14, Jesus dines in the home of a Pharisee. This is one of the many meal scenes in Luke's Gospel, with meals being socially defining occasions regarding who was considered "in" or "out" of one's community. On the one hand, Jesus heals the man with dropsy, a disability involving excess bodily fluids and inflammation (edema) caused by insatiable thirst. On the other hand, Jesus' intention was to challenge the Pharisees' understanding of the purpose of the Sabbath (14:3–5) and then to contrast their social conventions and values with that of the coming kingdom. The protocol for first-century client-patron relations clearly defined the rules of who invites whom, where each sits, what is then expected in return from such invitations, and so on. Jesus' two parables, of the wedding feast and the eschatological banquet, were intended to teach humility rather than to promote social status, to overturn the rules of you-invite-me-and-I-invite-you reciprocity, and to warn his hearers that the kingdom would include those at the bottom rather than at the top of the social, political, and religious hierarchy.

The main points of Jesus' teachings are brought home powerfully by his including the poor, the crippled, the lame, and the blind around the great banquet table (14:13, 21). These were the outcasts who had no status and were incapable of reciprocating the "generosity" of the host. For that very reason, social conventions would have dictated that they politely decline the invitation to begin with, so that Jesus insists that they need to be compelled to attend the banquet and carried in if necessary (14:23). What is truly astounding about this parable is the presence of people with clearly recognized disabilities at the *eschatological* banquet of the kingdom. So while Jesus' healing of people with disabilities would have confirmed some prophetic pronouncements that the blind, lame, and deaf would be cured on the coming Day of the Lord, in this case Jesus' inclusion of such people *just as they are* in the great banquet picks up on other prophetic themes about the coming kingdom involving the flourishing of all people not because we are physically cured but precisely because the social stigma of our disabilities no longer divides us (cf. Jer. 31:8–9; Mic. 4:6–7; Zeph. 3:19). In short, the restoration and redemption of Israel would include people like the eunuch and Zaccheus, not "fixed" so that they can conform to our social standards of beauty and desirability, but precisely as a testimony to the power of God to save all of us "normal" folk from our own discriminatory attitudes, inhospitable actions, and exclusionary social and political forms of life.

Does not the Holy Spirit still wish to do today what was accomplished two thousand years ago with this Ethiopian eunuch? Here is the redemption and restoration of one excluded geographically, racially, and physically. There is a massive revival occurring today on the African continent, and in many respects, the growing numbers of African Christians today can count themselves among the posterity of this Ethiopian official! But in a very real sense, we are still awaiting the day when the hospitality of the Spirit will be fully manifest in the church so that people with disabilities—those with physical, sensory, and intellectual differences—will be able to count themselves as descendents of this impaired eunuch. There are some indications that this is happening, for example in L'Arche communities where core members (who are people with disabilities) and assistants minister to each other in mutually transformative ways. Our prayer should be that more of us will be inspired by the Spirit of God to intentionally form fully inclusive communities that will be redemptive with good news for all people, both with and without disabilities.

20
The Spirit and Politics of (Paul's) Conversion

Acts 9:1-31

I F PAUL HAD KNOWN OF THE IMPAIRED EUNUCH, he would have empathized with him. While it is unclear what kind of physical infirmity, impairment, or disability Paul suffered, he indicated that he had learned to live with his condition, even to the point of recognizing that it was precisely in his bodily weaknesses that Christ was strong (see 2 Cor. 12:5–10; Gal. 4:13–14). Yet in this description of Paul's conversion, Luke is most interested neither in the physical healing—which blindness from the heavenly light some think may have left Paul with an ongoing visual impairment of some sort (cf. Gal. 6:11)—nor psychological transformation of one who was "still breathing threats and murder against the disciples of the Lord" (Acts 9:1). Instead, the focus is on how the persecutor of the saints from Jerusalem to Damascus became an instrument who would take the gospel to the ends of the earth.

In his own words, Paul said, "I am a Jew, born in Tarsus in Cilicia, a Hebrew born of Hebrews; as to the law, a Pharisee; as to zeal, a persecutor of the church; as to righteousness under the law, blameless" (Phil. 3:5–6). Although educated under Gamaliel (Acts 22:3), his zeal for the law motivated his sense of urgency in response to the Jesus sect rather than adoption of the wait-and-see attitude of his teacher. Paul sided with his fellow Hellenistic Jews against Stephen and other believers in Jesus, who were thought to have betrayed the way of the elders, and, perhaps as a member of the Sanhedrin council, "cast [his] vote against them when they were being condemned to death" (26:10).

On the Damascus Way, however, Paul was confronted with the risen Christ and filled with the Spirit (9:17) who had raised Jesus from the dead. Although the Acts narrative suggests that the sequence of events between his conversion and ministry initially in Damascus and then in Jerusalem occurred over a brief period, at least three years may have passed before his visit to Jerusalem (see Gal. 1:17–18). During this time, Paul reconsidered his entire worldview and theology in light of his encounter with Jesus. He became convinced that the message and ministry of Jesus about the renewal of Israel was vindicated by God through the Resurrection, which confirmed the crucified Galilean as the Messiah. In the process, like Stephen, Paul came to see that the messiahship of Jesus was relevant not only for the redemption of Israel but for the rest of the world as well.

It was this issue that separated Paul's ministry, at least at the outset, from those of the apostles. The Twelve were focused on evangelizing their fellow Judeans, and when the persecution dispersed the early Christian community into the countryside of Judea and Samaria, they remained in Jerusalem. They appointed Hellenistic Jews to care for the Hellenistic widows, and it was these deacons who first began to see the possibility that the renewal of Israel was not exclusive but perhaps inclusive of Samaritans, Ethiopians, and other Gentiles. Yes, Peter and John did participate in the mission to Samaria, but even after that Peter didn't think that the baptism of repentance for the forgiveness of sins and the gift of the Holy Spirit were for

Gentiles. Paul's recollection was that, even after fourteen years or more, the ministry of Peter, James, and John remained focused on the Jews to the point that they continued to exclude Gentiles from full table fellowship (Gal. 2:1, 7–14).

Paul the Hellenistic Jew, however, came to see that the message of the risen Christ was for the Jews first but also for the Gentiles (Rom. 1:17). More pointedly, the salvation of Israel was intimately linked with the salvation of the Gentiles. And if all of this was supposed to happen in the final Day of the Lord, the resurrection of Jesus announced that day had in some sense arrived! In fact, if the Gentiles were to be saved through Israel and her Messiah, it is also the case that Israel will finally be saved through the Gentiles (Rom. 11:25–36). Jesus' resurrection from the dead thus led not to the revolutionary overthrow of Roman imperial power but rather inaugurated the fulfillment of the promises made to Abraham that through his seed the Gentiles would be blessed. So the restored Israel's messianic community would not perpetuate the violence characteristic of "politics as usual" but would instead embody the peacefulness and forgiveness of sins characteristic of the eschatological body politic gathered around the resurrected Messiah.

The Lord commissioned Paul as "an instrument whom I have chosen to bring my name before Gentiles and kings and before the people of Israel" (Acts 9:15). Paul understood that bringing Jesus' name to the Gentiles involved establishing assemblies (congregations) in that name. The apostles had begun to do that in Jerusalem, and the early messianic community gave strong witness to the risen Christ through their mutuality, reciprocity, and loving fellowship. The dispersion of the messianic believers, however, led to the planting of new communities in Judea, Samaria, and toward the ends of the earth. Ironically, the one who had done his part in persecuting the followers of Jesus became one of those who would be most effective in multiplying messianic congregations around the Roman Empire. Not surprisingly, the apostolic leaders insisted that, in his evangelistic endeavors, Paul should not neglect the economic ministries that characterized the mission of the earliest believers and that he should "remember the poor" (which Paul said he was "eager to do"; Gal. 2:10).

Perhaps it was the universal implications of Jesus' messiahship that provoked the reaction to Paul's ministry, just as it was for precisely these same reasons that Paul (and other Jews) rejected Stephen's message. Both in Damascus and, later, in Jerusalem, his former Hellenistic Jewish colleagues turned on him (Acts 9:29), just as he had previously sought to imprison and put to death the messianic believers. Yet the fierce opposition to Paul should be quite understandable. He himself persecuted the Jesus followers because he saw this sectarian movement as a threat to Yahweh's covenant with the Jews. With Paul now preaching Jesus as the Messiah (Acts 9:22) who hadn't actually delivered the Jews from imperial domination, the question arose: what did this mean for the redemption of Israel? Further, if all Gentiles, even the Roman oppressors, could be saved through the Messiah's name, did that dispense with the covenant promises of God, and did that mean the Jews would now be assimilated into a much larger messianic community of Gentiles? But if so, didn't that signal the end of Israel as the uniquely chosen people of God? These are difficult but important questions that we will need to keep in mind as we continue to ask about what the Holy Spirit is doing in the world then and now.

21
Conversion and the Calling of the Spirit

Luke 5:1-11, 27-32; 9:21-27, 57-62; 12:49-53; 14:25-35

UKE CAREFULLY NARRATES PAUL'S CONVERSION and calling since it is Paul that becomes the major character in Acts from chapter 13 onward. At the same time, Paul's conversion reflects the major elements revealed in Jesus' call to discipleship in the Gospel of Luke. In what ways does Paul become the model convert and follower of Jesus?

First, God calls to repentance and commissions to the work of the kingdom especially sinners (Lk. 5:32). Simon Peter's conversion, which is important because of the central role he plays in Acts 1–12, involved a moment of recognizing himself as a sinner before Jesus (Lk. 5:8), and Levi's work as a tax collector was sufficient to classify him in the category of sinners (Lk. 5:30). We know from Paul's letters that he considered himself the chief of sinners (1 Tim. 1:15). The Holy Spirit calls and empowers sinners. We might now despise "those sinners," but only if we have become self-righteous—in which case, we remain no better than others (Lk. 18:9–14).

Second, conversion to Christ requires single-minded devotion in following him. Simon Peter and Levi almost literally did leave everything in order to follow Jesus (Lk. 5:11, 28). In Peter's case—and presumably those of his partners James and John—Jesus' invitation meant leaving his vocation as a fisherman behind. (In Acts, we find them stationed in Jerusalem rather than continuing to work out of the region of Lake Gennesaret.) It is also suggested that Levi ceased working as a tax collector, although we have no later evidence for that. The point Luke is emphasizing is that, whereas prior to Christian discipleship we pursue our economic well-being by trying to "gain the whole world," following Jesus means that we "profit" from adopting his way of life and "forfeit" the world's gains instead. (These are the economic terms of Lk. 9:25.)

We know that Paul continued his work as a tentmaker, which supported his missionary ventures (Acts 18:3). But even if Paul's conversion did not mean leaving his tentmaking behind, it did mean considering "everything as loss because of the surpassing value of knowing Christ Jesus my Lord. For his sake I have suffered the loss of all things, and I regard them as rubbish, in order that I may gain Christ" (Phil. 3:8). No doubt Ananias (not the same person as the one we met earlier in Acts 5) also warned Paul that God's call would require not only severing his attachments to the world but also being prepared to suffer for the sake of the gospel (Acts 9:16). In short, while conversion to Christ may or may not involve the abandonment of one's former vocation, Jesus' warning remains apropos regarding the cost of discipleship: "None of you can become my disciple if you do not give up all your possessions" (Lk. 14:33).

The third element is a radicalization of the second: conversion requires forsaking all one has, even one's family. If one's work provided for one's material needs, then one's family and kin were the wider support network when the provisions of work were insufficient. To be ready to forsake one's family in addition to one's vocation and possessions would be suicidal in a peasant economy. Yet that is what conversion demanded. This goes beyond simply not saying farewell (9:61); rather, it means being prepared to be set against one's closest kin if they were unwilling also to follow Jesus (12:52–53; 14:26).

We do not know too much about Paul's immediate family except that he appears to have had a sister (and her family) in Jerusalem (Acts 23:16). Yet we also know that he had been committed to the cause of keeping the Jewish faith, and this was expressed in his working closely with other like-minded and zealous Hellenistic Jews to preserve the covenant. But conversion to Christ set him against these Jewish groups with whom he had been formerly aligned (9:29). Following Jesus did indeed bring about division and separation from his former allegiances (Lk. 12:51–52).

Yet conversion to the way of Jesus did not leave one alone. Instead, it brought about a new family, a new people of God, bound together in loyalty to the Messiah. Here was a new kinship, manifest initially in the community of equals gathered around the apostle's teaching, the daily breaking of bread together, and the mutual sharing so that none had need (Acts 2:42–47; 4:32–35). As we see, Paul simply carried the apostolic message outward from Jerusalem and Judea and in the process established many such congregations and assemblies around the Roman Empire. Hence, to forsake all, even one's family, for the sake of Christ did result in the gaining of much more, even an extended family constituted otherwise of aliens and strangers.

Finally, conversion not only meant renouncing the world for a new identity and community, but it also brought about a new purpose: that of proclaiming the kingdom (Lk. 9:26, 60, 62). Radical discipleship is required because of the radical commitment needed to sustain the work of the kingdom. Rather than seeking the approval of the world (14:7–14) or being consumed by the world's demands (14:18–20), the work of the kingdom invites us to relinquish our own goals in order to restore, renew, and redeem Israel and to establish the reign of Yahweh. Paul knew from the beginning of his encounter with Jesus that he had been recommissioned by the God of Israel to take the Good News "before Gentiles and kings and before the people of Israel" (Acts 9:15). The proclamation of the kingdom, then, inevitably included this political dimension.

Luke's notion of conversion involves not merely the salvation of souls but also radical discipleship and commitment. The cross is not understood merely as a penal substitutionary atonement for the sins of humankind. Rather than the death of Jesus exemplifying God's triumph over the problem of human sin and guilt, the cross symbolizes the way of the Messiah, his willingness to confront the deceitful, unjust, and violent systems of this world, even to the point of death. More to the point, the cross is the way of life to which Christian conversion is invited: "If any want to become my followers, let them deny themselves and take up their cross daily and follow me" (Lk. 9:23).

What is the Holy Spirit doing today? Nothing more or less than what he did in the lives of Peter, Levi, and Paul: he is calling sinners to repentance, enabling the renunciation of all ties that would enmesh us with the systems of the world, empowering the proclamation of the kingdom, and sustaining faithfulness in the way of Jesus, even to the point of death if necessary. Paul's conversion signaled the death of one devoted to a parochial view of God's covenant promises and the resurrection of one now inspired to work for the redemption of Jews and Gentiles in Christ through the power of the Spirit.

22
Resurrection and the Power of the Spirit

Acts 9:32-43; 20:7-12; Luke 7:11-17

E CAN NOW SEE how the radical discipleship of the way of Jesus simply foreshadowed the even more radical salvation of God at the resurrection. Thus, from the beginning of their Spirit-empowered ministries, the apostles bore witness not only to the resurrection of Jesus (Acts 2:31; 4:33) but also to the hope that "in Jesus there is the resurrection of the dead" (4:2). They had come to see that Jesus' resurrection confirmed his message regarding the renewal of Israel and that this redemption involved not only the proclamation of the gospel to the poor and the healing of the sick but also the raising of the dead (see Lk. 7:22)— all anticipating the general resurrection to come. Yet, as with the hope of Israel promulgated by the prophets, resurrection through the power of the Spirit was never understood only as an individual affair but concerned the corporate people of God (see Ezek. 37:1– 14). Such a socially and communally oriented understanding of the resurrection power of the Spirit can be discerned in three biblical narratives: Jesus' raising of the widow of Nain's son in Luke 7, Peter's raising of Tabitha in Acts 9, and Paul's raising of Eutychus in Acts 20.

Jesus' encounter with the widow at Nain in Luke chapter 7 is set within a public context: a large crowd following him into Nain meets up with a large crowd of mourners in funeral procession at the city gates. The former is exuberant following the healing of the centurion's daughter (7:1–10), while the latter is grieving with and for this widowed woman who, with the passing of her only son, is now truly left alone in the world. She no longer possesses social status (social standing being determined in part by one's posterity), is bereft of economic livelihood (elderly parents were dependent on their grown children), and lacks political representation (it was the men who ruled from the city gates).

Jesus appears to have recognized her plight and "had compassion for her" (7:13). Transgressing purity laws in touching the bier (7:14), Jesus speaks life into the young man and returns him to his mother. The marvelousness of this encounter is only partially that of the bodily resuscitation (a more appropriate term than resurrection, which technically continues to apply to Jesus alone, since all other resuscitations have, eventually, been followed by death). The other part has to do with the "resurrection" of life for the mother—the restoration of her social status, the renewal of her economic livelihood, and the reestablishment of her political representation at the city gates. Beyond that, the resuscitation of the young man also returns another healthy body desperately needed for the peasant economy of Nain. In short, the power of the Spirit works not only a biological miracle but also a social miracle in reinvigorating a family and an entire community.

Even as Jesus' raising the son of the widow of Nain identified him as being the prophet anticipated by Israel (7:16) in the tradition of Elijah and Elisha (see their own feats of raising the dead in 1 Kgs. 17:20–24; 2 Kgs. 4:32–37), so also this event serves as the paradigm for the "resurrections" accomplished through Peter and Paul in Acts. Peter's narrative (Acts 9:32–12:19) is an interlude between the conversion of Paul (Acts 9:1–31) and Paul's emergence to prominence later in the mission to the Gentiles (Acts 13 and following). In the meanwhile, recall that Stephen and Philip had already led the way in taking the gospel to Samaria (Acts 8). Here Peter himself is finally following the lead of the Spirit out of Jerusalem into the surrounding regions of Judea.

The irony of the Tabitha narrative (Acts 9:32–43) reveals how the Spirit accomplishes the purposes of God regardless of the plans of human beings. Recall that, although previously the apostles had reserved for themselves the prerogative of the ministry of the word and commissioned the seven deacons to serve the tables of widows (6:3–6), at least two of the seven turned out to lead more effective evangelistic and missionary ministries than the apostles, at least with regard to Hellenistic Jews and Samaritans. Now Peter finds himself called to minister to a group of mourning widows—which probably involved Hellenistic Jews, with Tabitha herself known in Greek as Dorcas—and it appears that they were expecting more from him than just his ministry of preaching.

It turns out that Tabitha had been a benefactress for a community of widows in Joppa (9:36, 39). A believer of some means, she appears to have modeled her life after that of Barnabas and the early Christian community of equals (4:32–37), giving to others out of her own abundance and caring and providing especially for widows in the village. Her death jeopardized the stability of other lives and led them to seek the life-giving power of God, perhaps not only for her sake but also for that of the whole community (9:38). As Jesus' raising the widow's young man resulted in the renewal of the town of Nain, so here Peter's raising of Tabitha restores hope to the marginalized and dispossessed of Joppa.

Fast-forwarding to Troas (Acts 20:5–6), we find that Paul's raising Eutychus from the dead occurs also in a communal setting wherein the believers had gathered on the first day of the week to break bread (20:7). Unlike Tabitha, who was of some means, in this case the disciples of Troas squeezed into a small third-floor "apartment" (20:9), perhaps the home of one of the believers. Apparently the meeting went late into the night, and Paul's droning on and on did nothing to help Eutychus stay awake. Unfortunately for him, he fell out of his window seat and died. Luckily for Paul, the Spirit's power to raise the dead was available that evening, and the community, with Eutychus, was able to joyously celebrate the Lord's Supper together before disbanding at dawn (20:11).[6]

The "resurrections" of Tabitha and Eutychus legitimated, respectively, the ministries of Peter (to the Jews) and Paul (to the Gentiles) as being authorized and empowered by the same Spirit who raised the dead through Jesus. So while bodily resurrections are no insignificant events, in Luke's narrative they serve to mark the messianic activities of Jesus and his appointed servants. Further, as I have attempted to show, although resurrections (and resuscitations) involved particular bodies—that of the young man of Nain or Tabitha or Eutychus—their relevance will be misunderstood if viewed only as biological miracles. Rather, in each case, the Spirit's bringing the dead to life has wider social and communal implications and reverberations.

This invites us to consider how some of our quests for miracles like resurrected bodies may be misguided. What is more important is the degree to which we are responding to the Spirit's empowering work to act transformatively in the world so that processes of death and destruction are reversed as we both proclaim and enact the good news of Jesus' message. If whole communities are being affected in ways that foster life, health, and shalom, then in those cases, we can acknowledge that the resurrection power of the Spirit has been at work, even through our mortal lives and bodies.

PART SIX

The Gentiles and the Holy Spirit

23
"God Shows No Partiality"! Jews, Gentiles, and the Spirit

Acts 10:1-11:15

THE CORNELIUS NARRATIVE IN ACTS is the gate that opens the "floods" of the gospel to flow out to the Gentile world. In one sense, the entirety of Luke's story so far, going all the way back to the beginning of the life of Jesus, has been anticipating this moment. At the presentation of Jesus shortly after his birth, Simeon rejoiced that God allowed him to see the salvation "prepared in the presence of all peoples, a light for revelation to the Gentiles" (Lk. 2:31–32), and the launch of the public ministry of Jesus was announced by the Baptist's proclamation that "all flesh shall see the salvation of God" (3:6).

Until now, the apostolic leadership has remained primarily in Jerusalem (Acts 8:2) and appears to have been reluctant to proclaim the gospel to the Gentiles. Yes, they were aware that the covenantal promises to Abraham brought with them blessings for "all the families of the earth" (3:25), but it was left up to Hellenistic Jews like Stephen and Philip to clearly point out that God's dwelling place was not limited to the temple (7:46–50) and to actively evangelize beyond the borders of Jerusalem. This being the case, God would act again to bring about the promise of the gift of the Spirit in order that his followers could be empowered to be witnesses "in Jerusalem, in all Judea and Samaria, and to the ends of the earth" (1:8). If on the Day of Pentecost the Spirit was poured out on Jews, proselytes, and others from all around the Mediterranean, then on the day of Cornelius's encounter with Peter, the Spirit would be poured out on the Gentiles, this time in anticipation of the ongoing outpourings of the Spirit on all who would be willing to receive him.

Yet the story of Cornelius's conversion is important because of its function in the broader Lukan narrative and because it reveals a God who "shows no partiality" (10:34) and a Spirit who makes no distinction (11:12). Here was a man whose life manifested all of the characteristics of Jewish piety: "He was a devout man who feared God with all his household; he gave alms generously to the people and prayed constantly to God" (10:2); more specifically, he is also said to be "an upright [from the Greek *dikaios*, meaning "righteous" or "just"] and God-fearing man, who is well spoken of by the whole Jewish nation" (10:22). Peter's response to Cornelius was that "your prayer has been heard and your alms have been remembered before God" (10:31).

How is it that a Gentile can be such a person of prayer apart from the specific revelation given to Jews or through Christ? Is it possible that Cornelius could have been an upright or righteous person even before hearing the gospel? Does God hear the prayers of all people, even if they are made without knowledge of the name or person of Jesus? The traditional answer is that God heard Cornelius's prayer and thus sent Peter to proclaim the gospel to him and his household. But does this mean that the only way God answers the prayers of those who cry out to him is to send a missionary and that therefore all unevangelized people have never cried out to God? Even if we answer yes to both questions, that still does not explain how Cornelius could have been an upright or righteous man who loved God (as manifest in his praying constantly) and, in effect, loved his neighbor as himself (as testified to by the Jewish people; cf. Lk. 10:27).

A more plausible response would be to see that the God who shows no partiality is the God who judges impartially as well, condemning unrepentant sinners but also accepting "in every nation anyone who fears him and does what is right" (Acts 10:34–35). To fear God and do what is right is not a merely human accomplishment; rather, these are works of the Holy Spirit, who hovered over the deep at the dawn of creation (Gen. 1:2), who is the life-breath of every creature and human being (Job 34:14–15; Ps. 104.29–30; Gen. 2:7), and from whose presence no one can ever successfully escape (Ps. 139:7–10). The Spirit who Luke says has been poured out on all flesh is the same Spirit of whom Paul writes, who continues to groan with the creation and with us in anticipation of the redemption and reconciliation of all things in the love of God in Christ (Rom. 8:22–23, 26–27, 35–39).

Thus is it possible that the unevangelized are not beyond the workings of the Spirit of God? Is it possible that the prayers of the unevangelized also rise up as a memorial before God and that God has his own ways of dealing with and accepting those who have constantly sought him, even apart from missionaries? This does not mean that we should cease and desist from the great commission. Rather, we should respond to the Spirit's promptings to go forth simply because that may be one of God's chosen means to respond to the prayers of those who call on his name for salvation. Peter's obedience gave him the opportunity to declare the forgiveness of sins to Cornelius (10:43), which provided assurance that his prayers had indeed been answered.

In Cornelius's case, Peter was not the only instrument of evangelism; instead, Cornelius was also an instrument for the conversion of Peter. This leading apostle had followed the call of Philip into Samaria and then ministered in Lydda and Joppa, and his itinerant ministry had led him to stay in the home of Simon, a tanner (Acts 9:43). This progression shows that he was by now open to at least associating with those formerly considered unclean (tanners, by profession, lived in violation of Jewish purity laws). However, it took a thrice-repeated vision of the Spirit of God—who, Luke says, continues to speak through visions (2:17)—to convince Peter that the laws prohibiting association with Gentiles had been overcome in Christ (10:28). Beyond that, it also took the outpouring of the Spirit on Cornelius and his household to reveal that such associations were now not just with acquaintances or neighbors but also with those whom "God has given . . . the repentance that leads to life" (11:18). Peter was converted from being merely a preacher of peace in Jesus (10:36) to being one who embodied and lived out the peace of Jesus to all people—even to those whom he had formerly considered unclean—by the power of the Holy Spirit.

Finally, note that Cornelius was a centurion, a high-ranking Roman public and military official. Yet Peter came to him "preaching peace by Jesus Christ" (10:36). This was the good news that reconciled not only Jews and Gentiles but also enemies.

Peter's testimony convinced other skeptical Jewish believers (11:2–3), at least for the moment, that Jewish-Christian fellowship was indeed possible. This watershed event would lead later on to Saint Paul's declaration that Jews and Gentiles "have access in one Spirit to the Father. So then you are no longer strangers and aliens, but you are citizens with the saints and also members of the household of God" (Eph. 2:18–19). Yet the question still remains: was this what Jesus envisioned in his preaching the gospel of the kingdom and the renewal of Israel?

24
Kingdom Work: Restoring Israel—
Calling the Nations!

Luke 6:12-19; 9:1-6; 10:1-24

*W*ITH JESUS, the restoration and renewal of Israel and the preaching of the kingdom were connected. We have already seen how the twelve apostles were intended to play a key role in ushering in the kingdom. Jesus commissioned the Twelve with a threefold task: (1) to proclaim the coming kingdom, (2) to heal the sick, and (3) to cast out demons (Lk. 9:1–2).

The mission of the Twelve was nothing less than a participation in the Spirit-empowered mission of the Messiah to preach good news to the poor, release the captives and the oppressed, and proclaim the coming kingdom (4:18–19). Thus the healings and exorcisms were connected not only in terms of Jesus' intentions to banish all oppression—physical and spiritual oppression are often intertwined—from the coming reign of God but also as concrete signs and manifestations that God's rule was appearing in his ministry and that of his "sent ones" (apostles). Positively understood, the arrival of the kingdom would be characterized by the fellowship of a reconciled community, the mutual sharing that provided for the needs of the community, and the experience of the forgiveness of sins apart from the temple sacrifices and the mediation of the priesthood.

Yet from the beginning, Luke provides clear indications that the renewal of Israel involves the salvation of the nations beyond Israel as well. Whereas Matthew records Jesus' prohibition, "Go nowhere among the Gentiles, and enter no town of the Samaritans" (10:5), Luke, who writes in hindsight of Philip's mission to the Samaritans and the conversions of the Ethiopian eunuch and Cornelius's household, leaves this out of his accounts altogether. Further, whereas Matthew simply has Jesus instructing the apostles to allow their peace to rest on the homes that receive them (10:13), Luke has Jesus commanding his sent ones to proclaim peace (Lk. 10:5). Peace, as we have already seen on various occasions (1:79; 2:14; 7:50; 8:48; 19:38, 42), can never be only partially present; if peace is to accompany the renewal of Israel, then righteousness and justice will have to be meted out to all the nations as well—otherwise, if there is discord, unrighteousness, or injustice anywhere, there can be no shalom for Israel either. Thus did Jesus intend his apostles to rule and reign with him according to the values of the kingdom rather than according to the authoritarian styles of the Gentiles (22:25–27). Most indicative of Jesus' inclusion of the Gentile nations with the restoration of Israel, however, is the sending out of the seventy/seventy-two only in the Gospel of Luke (10:1).[7]

In sum, what is unique to Luke's universal horizon, when compared with the other synoptic Gospels, is that Jesus authorized the apostles to go, without limiting them to evangelizing only their fellow Jews, and further appoints seventy/seventy-two for the task of proclaiming and doing the works of the kingdom even while urging them all to pray and "ask the Lord of the harvest to send out laborers into his harvest" (Lk. 10:2). In this context, there is no need to assume that the gospel would be limited only to the Jews. Further, even for Jewish listeners, those who rejected the apostles of Jesus would find themselves excluded from the kingdom (10:10–16); they could not count on their covenant status to secure their place in the renewed Israel. After all, those who rejected the apostles were rejecting Jesus' message and, along with it, the offer of Jesus' Father, the "Lord of heaven and earth" (10:21), whom the Son himself represented. So, while Jesus saw the connection between the renewal of Israel and the coming of the kingdom, it is also fair to say that the renewal of Israel was not exclusive of the salvation of the Gentiles.

Over two thousand years later, Gentile readers of Luke and of this book may wonder what the big deal is. We must not underemphasize, however, how drastic of an idea it was to the original Jews that the restoration of Israel involved those who were not Israel. Similarly, I wonder if those of us who now consider our membership among the people of God as secure might be challenged to ask if there are others, those outside the pale of who we might think are among the elect, whom God may nevertheless count as his own. We have already mentioned some classes of people on whom the Spirit has been, is being, and will be poured out—the poor, the oppressed, people with disabilities, and other who are not "us." The earliest apostles went very reluctantly outside their borders of comfort. Contemporary Christians also often do not venture out to mix with "others." But if the Spirit is truly calling *all* nations, then we should be ready both to go to "them" and to receive "others" into our midst so that we also might be transformed in the process.

25

"Cast Out the Evil One"! Sorcery and the Spirit/s

Acts 13:1-12; 19:8-20

*W*E HAVE PREVIOUSLY SEEN the Spirit's power manifest over the magical arts when Philip went into Samaria and confronted Simon the sorcerer (Acts 8). As we move out further from Jerusalem into the wider Roman Empire, we now see the magical arts manifest as a syncretistic phenomenon combining Jewish traditions, Greco-Roman religions, and local practices. In Ephesus (Acts 19), we come upon a hotbed of religious activity—Jewish exorcists, Jewish and Gentile practitioners of the magical arts, and the worship of the goddess Artemis—and in Cyprus (Acts 13), we find a Jewish magician, Bar-Jesus, serving as an advisor to a Gentile proconsul. Although Jews were forbidden to dabble in magic, the presence in Cyprus of someone like Bar-Jesus, also known as the "wise one" (etymologically linked to the name "Elymas"), would not have been surprising given the long tradition of such *magoi* in the Gentile world (e.g., Pharaoh's magicians in Exod. 7–9, Balaam in Num. 22–24, and the Persian astrologers who followed the star of Jesus in Matt. 2).

The case of Bar-Jesus further illustrates the seamless interconnections between magic, religion, politics, and economics in the ancient Near East. Unlike the separation of church and state, of religion and politics, which has become constitutionally standard in America at least, the first-century Greco-Roman and Hellenistic world viewed magic and religion as keys to power (in the political domain) and wealth (in economic life). Bar-Jesus clearly felt that if Sergius Paulus converted to become a follower of the Way of Jesus, his proconsul would be lost as a patron. In Ephesus, the fifty thousand silver coins' worth—each denarius being a full day's wage!—of books about the magic arts that were burned suggests that many had accumulated a great deal of wealth using these practices. While the motives of the seven sons of Sceva are not clearly specified, parallels with the Samaritan episode indicate that they may have been similarly motivated as was Simon Magus: to obtain power over the spiritual realm for the sake of profit.

There are several levels at which we can and should understand the two "power encounters" described in the texts under consideration. At the interpersonal level, Paul's contest with Bar-Jesus, the "son of the devil" and "enemy of all righteousness" (Acts 13:10), confirms his apostolic credentials as equivalent to that manifest by Peter in his encounter with the Satan-filled Ananias and Sapphira (5:3). Further, the declaration of the evil spirits to the sons of Sceva—that "Jesus I know, and Paul I know; but who are you?" (19:15)—further legitimizes Paul's authority in connection with Jesus. Just as Jesus cast out demons by the power of the Spirit (10:38), so also does Paul overcome the wiles of the devil by the same Spirit (13:9–11).

At the level of the Acts narrative, however, these two passages reveal how Christian faith is established in pagan (Gentile) regions previously under the grip of other spiritual powers. Bar-Jesus' blindness led to the conversion of the proconsul (13:12), and as news about the sons of Sceva spread quickly, "everyone was awestruck; and the name of the Lord Jesus was praised. . . . So the word of the

Lord grew mightily and prevailed" (19:17, 20). The spread of faith in Jesus from Antioch, where Paul began his missionary ventures at the instigation of the Holy Spirit (13:2), to Cyprus and then later to Ephesus is noteworthy given the central location of the island on the Mediterranean trade route and the importance of Ephesus as an imperial city. With regard to the latter, Luke suggests that the gospel does not seem to have made much headway even after two years of persistent ministry by Paul (19:9–10), but the breakthrough occurred with the sons of Sceva incident. Any success is dependent, of course, on the work of the Spirit, who commissioned the missionary venture of Paul, just as the Spirit did for Peter (on the Day of Pentecost) and Jesus (at his baptism). Empowered by the Spirit, Paul encounters and prevails over the spirits of Cyprus and Ephesus.

In the larger scheme of Luke-Acts, the conflict with evil spirits is a subtheme of the major plot. Paul is specifically said to have proclaimed God's kingdom at the beginning of his mission at Ephesus (19:8). The experience of the sons of Sceva shows that, while they were interested in expanding their repertoire of exorcistic formulas, the coming of the kingdom had to do with the person of Jesus himself. The casting out of demons depends not on the formulaic recitation of Jesus' name but on the proper representation of his personal authority. And just as Jesus indicated, "If . . . I cast out the demons, then the kingdom of God has come to you" (Lk. 11:20), so also in the cases of the disciples—Peter, Philip, and Paul (respectively, Acts 5:15–16; 8:7; 19:11–12)—the casting out of demons heralded the presence of the Spirit of Jesus and the in-breaking of the kingdom as well. These episodes reveal the political dimensions of "spiritual warfare," showing clearly what happens when the coming kingdom invades the power structures of the present world.

Yet there remains a fine line between the authentic enculturation of the gospel and its syncretism with local traditions. In the religious culture of the first century, Greco-Roman religions were fused with indigenous religio-cultural practices, often resulting in syncretistic amalgamations of the magical arts. In the popular realm, the quest for miraculous healing, economic relief, and political power was often met through religio-political leaders (like Bar-Jesus) or the village shaman (note that Sceva was said to be a Jewish priest; 19:14). Christianity captured the popular imagination, it seems, at least in part because the apostles were able to meet the expectations of Gentiles and outperform the pagan magical artists. Thus Paul's healing powers were mediated through handkerchiefs and aprons (19:12) just as Peter's were effected through his shadow (5:15) and Jesus' through the hem of his garments (Lk. 6:19; 8:44). Yet even believers in the Messiah (perhaps many being new converts) continued to practice magic (Acts 19:19), until the sons of Sceva incident registered the gospel truth that the power of Jesus resided not in the mere utterance of his name but in the properly delegated representation of his kingdom authority.

Similar challenges remain today, especially in the expansion of Christianity in the Global South (Asia, Africa, and Latin America). On the one hand, there are mass conversions to Christian faith when people encounter the power of God to heal, exorcise evil spirits, and deliver from oppression. On the other hand, even after conversion, many continue to consult the local shaman or inappropriately blend their new faith with previous religio-cultural practices. When does enculturation or contextualization devolve into syncretism? Do the many tongues of the Spirit both enable the translation of the gospel into the many languages and cultures of the world and yet simultaneously threaten to dissolve the distinctiveness of the gospel in a pluralistic world? Might the exorcism of evil spirits be compromised in the unintended mingling of religious practices?

From a political standpoint, though, the challenge is to take seriously the biblical principalities and powers without being naive about demonizing actual governments, organizations, or sociopolitical-economic systems. Too often we associate economic poverty, political corruption, or social underdevelopment and unrest with pagan religions or with demonic activity. Doing so, however, overlooks the fact that all of these realities exist even within supposedly "Christian" contexts even while they foster a demon-behind-every-tree mentality that does not take responsibility for what can be changed. The key is to pray against the powers but simultaneously bear witness to Christ in the power of the Spirit in ways that make a political or public difference in the world.

26
Satan, the Demonic, and Empire

Luke 4:1-14, 31-37; 8:26-39; 9:37-42, 49-50; 11:14-26

HEN THE DISCIPLES COMPLAINED about someone outside the circle of Jesus' followers casting out demons in his name, Jesus responded, "Do not stop him; for whoever is not against you is for you" (Lk. 9:50). Yet, when his opponents accused him of casting out demons by the power of Beelzebub (synonymous with Satan), he answered, "Every kingdom divided against itself becomes a desert, and house falls on house. If Satan also is divided against himself, how will his kingdom stand?—for you say that I cast out the demons by Beelzebul. Now if I cast out the demons by Beelzebul, by whom do your exorcists cast them out? Therefore they will be your judges" (11:17–19). It appears the sons of Sceva were seeking their own personal gain so that their attempted exorcisms were unsuccessful because they were not accompanied by the presence and authority of Jesus, God's representative sent to establish the kingdom.

Jesus' first recorded encounter with the devil reveals how his mission to redeem Israel and usher in the kingdom confronted the kingdom of darkness. Whereas Israel spent forty years in the wilderness in rebellion against God, Jesus spent forty days in the desert seeking the will of God. Whereas Israel did not rely on God's provision of the manna, was disobedient to God's commands, and put God to the test repeatedly, Jesus resisted each of these temptations, thereby establishing the foundations for the restoration of the nation. Whereas Israel rebelled against God and "grieved his holy spirit" (Isa. 63:10), Jesus was led by the Spirit into and within the desert and, "filled with the power of the Spirit, returned to Galilee" (Lk. 4:14) to continue his mission. Even though Satan promised all of the kingdoms of the world (4:5–6), Jesus rejected that and instead trusted Yahweh's promises to grant him the nations (see Ps. 2:8). He was gearing up for a frontal attack against the powers of the devil, a battle to neutralize the devil's armor and weapons and to plunder the kingdom of darkness (11:22).

Fresh from his overcoming the temptations of the devil, Jesus proceeded by the power of the Spirit to release the captives, deliver the oppressed, and proclaim the year of the Lord's favor (4:18–19). And the devil's minions realized that his appearance anticipated their torment and destruction (4:34; 8:36). Jesus cast out evil spirits first in Capernaum and then the surrounding regions of Galilee (4:41; 6:18) before heading across the lake to the Gentile region of Gerasa (8:22, 26). The demoniac he encountered was possessed by thousands—a legion (8:30)—of evil spirits. Perhaps he was the scapegoat cast out of the community (into the tombs and the wild) whose life represented the disorder (expressed in his nakedness) experienced by the Gerasene people because of the oppression they suffered under Roman rule, taxation, and exploitation (symbolized by the guards, chains, and shackles with which he was bound; 8:29). In this case, the casting out of Legion into the abyss denoted the overthrow of imperial domination and tyranny and established Jesus' universal authority and power beyond the borders of Israel.

More specifically the deliverance of the demoniac announced the arrival of the kingdom. As Jesus said later, "If it is by the finger of God that I cast out the demons, then the kingdom of God has come to you" (Lk. 11:20). Whereas Beelzebub is ruler over his kingdom of demons (11:15), Jesus threatens to turn it into a desert by heralding the arrival of king Yahweh over the restored nation of Israel and the renewed world of the Gentiles; and whereas the devil seeks to maintain his oppressive control over the world (his castle, 11:21), Jesus arrives by the power of the Spirit in order to redeem and restore the world and its inhabitants to its rightful owner.

So on the one hand, the devil and his minions afflict the world physically (as reflected in their responsibility for specific cases of epileptic seizures and muteness; 9:38–39; 11:14). On the other hand, the devil's works debilitated entire families and communities. Within the kingdom horizon of Luke, it was a case of the kingdom of darkness versus the kingdom of light (cf. Acts 26:18), with the battles being fought at every level ranging from that of imperial Rome, the Jewish leadership, regional authorities (like those in Gerasa), and local communities (like that of the isle of Cyprus, under the leadership of the proconsul Sergius Paulus and his advisor, Bar-Jesus; Acts 13:6) to that of each family and every individual. Jesus came by the power of the Spirit to declare and establish the kingdom; it was up to those who were delivered at each level, however, to embrace the representatives of the kingdom or risk being reinvaded by the principalities and powers seven times more evil than those before (Lk. 11:26).

Similarly, today it is up to us to discern, following the guiding of the Holy Spirit, when encountering a situation of epilepsy (or mental illness or schizophrenia) or deafness or muteness or economic depression or political oppression or, perhaps simultaneously with any of the above or much more, whether evil spirits are involved. Regardless of the situation, we must always be alert to the presence and activity of the demonic when there is opposition to the kingdom of Christ, of his righteousness, peace, and shalom. Thus did the Apostle Paul write, "Our struggle is not against enemies of blood and flesh, but against the rulers, against the authorities, against the cosmic powers of this present darkness, against the spiritual forces of evil in the heavenly places" (Eph. 6:12). Sometimes the battle is lost because those who enter the fray are not doing so for the right reasons (e.g., the sons of Sceva) and are thus not with Christ but against him (Lk. 11:23). Other times, the followers of Jesus as the Messiah may simply lack faith (9:40–41; Luke omits mention that the disciples neglected either prayer or fasting, as indicated in Mk. 9:29). Yet when properly commissioned by Christ and empowered by his Spirit, the kingdom advances amid reports that, "Lord, in your name even the demons submit to us!" (Lk. 10:17).

This means that we also can be agents of the renewal of Israel and the arrival of the kingdom, delivering the oppressed, opposing the powers of darkness in control of the castle gates, and even resisting the oppressive and destructive ways of empire. No wonder that "even the demons believe—and shudder" (Jas. 2:19). Why wouldn't they? The lives of many, not to mention the kingdoms of this world currently under the sway of the evil one (1 Jn. 5:19), are at stake. And the same Spirit who anointed Jesus to go about "doing good and healing all who were oppressed by the devil" (Acts 10:38) continues to empower the works of Jesus' followers today, so that through them, Jesus, who has gone to be with the Father, can do even greater things than he did while in the flesh (Jn. 14:12).

27
The Spirit's Universal Work

Acts 13:13-15:35

N THE WILDERNESS and then in his life and ministry, Jesus defeated the devil, lived a righteous life in obedience to God, and pronounced the forgiveness of sins—all acts related to the salvation of Israel. However, the problem was that most people of his day, including the Jewish leadership, did not understand that the renewal of Israel brought with it the rule and reign of the Lord over the world, including the extension of God's saving covenant with the Gentiles as well. As the messianic community expanded from Jerusalem into Judea and Samaria and beyond, the disciples grappled with the implications of this growth, even as they encountered resistance especially from the Jewish leaders who perceived such developments as threatening the fragility of the Jewish diasporic existence.

In Luke's account of Paul's preaching in Antioch of Pisidia, we see how these early followers of Jesus began to understand the relationship between Israel and the salvation of the Gentiles. Addressing both Jews and Gentile God-fearers in the synagogue (Acts 13:16, 26), Paul begins first with God's election of Israel. The deliverance from Egypt, the conquest of Canaan, and the appointment of judges and then kings are all acts of Yahweh culminating in the Davidic covenant and promise of the messianic Savior in his line (13:17–23). Although he was executed as an innocent man, his resurrection from the dead fulfilled the promises made to David

(13:27–37) and vindicated his life and ministry, especially the forgiveness of sins made available in his name (13:38). But even more unbelievable (13:41) and, for the Jews, scandalous was that "by this Jesus *everyone who believes* [not just Jews!] is set free from all those sins from which you could not be freed by the law of Moses" (13:39, emphasis added). The Gentiles who heard this offer of forgiveness "were glad and praised the word of the Lord" (13:48) and, as promised by Peter on the Day of Pentecost (2:38), "were filled with joy and with the Holy Spirit" (13:52). The forgiveness of sins, the righteousness, peace, and joy manifest in the life of Christ and the overcoming of the kingdom of darkness in his name were all available to any who believed and were willing to receive—Jews and Gentiles. More precisely, it is the rebuilding of the house of David, the restoration of Israel, that is the means through which the rest of the world might be saved (15:16–17).

But just as the Jewish leaders resisted the ministry of Jesus and the apostles in Jerusalem and just as the Hellenistic Jews who were zealous for the ministry of the temple rejected the ministry of Stephen, so also the Jewish and Gentile leaders at Antioch in Pisidia and Iconium opposed Paul's message (13:45, 50; 14:2, 5, 19). The Gentile leadership may have been concerned about the loss of patronage at their local temples or about upsetting the cult of Caesar. The Jews, on the other hand, may have been alerted by the faction from Judea who came up to Antioch saying, "Unless you are circumcised according to the custom of Moses, you cannot be saved" (15:1). Perhaps they were envious (13:45) that the covenant promises of Moses and David were being extended to the Gentiles without any requirement to keep the Mosaic law or to undergo circumcision, the sign of the covenant (15:5, 24). Further, if indeed the renewal of Israel now included the salvation of the Gentiles, then there could no longer be punishment for Israel's oppressors, and without such judgment, there would be no vindication of Israel as God's specially elected people. Did not such an unconditional acceptance and even election of the Gentiles as part of the people of God (13:48; 15:7) threaten to undo the covenant itself?

Paul found himself being stretched along two fronts. God, who had called him "to be a light for the Gentiles . . . [and to] bring salvation to the ends of the earth" (13:47, alluding to Isa. 49:6), had empowered him with the Spirit to preach the good news to those who had been without the law. So, for example, when preaching to the peasant villagers at Lystra, Paul spoke about the Creator of the world, who also provided for his creatures (14:15–17). It was this God who was now intent on lavishing on them the unconditional forgiveness of sins and eternal life in his kingdom. However, this message seemed, to Jewish leaders and purists, too discontinuous from the covenant promises made to Moses and David. There was no longer any need for the priesthood and the temple sacrifices, and the very foundations of the law now appeared to be undermined.

It turns out that things were actually as "bad" as they thought. Not only had God chosen the Gentiles (13:48; 15:14), but God had also seen fit to give Gentiles the Holy Spirit, to cleanse their hearts by faith, and to no longer make a distinction between Jew and Gentile (15:8–9). Even more, Peter insisted that, rather than the Gentiles participating in the salvation promised to the Jews, it was the other way around—that the salvation of the Gentiles was the norm, and that even Jews "will be saved through the grace of the Lord Jesus, *just as they* [Gentiles] *will*" (15:11, emphasis added). And instead of discerning these developments as being in accordance with the Scriptures, the prophets are now read (retrospectively, it would appear) as agreeing with God's acting to save the Gentiles (15:15).

Although Jews were only now understanding God's generosity, it had always been a part of God's plan, from the very beginning (15:18, 21). Yet through all this, the apostolic leaders came to see through the Holy Spirit (15:28) that, while the Gentiles could be saved just as they were (without fully converting to become Jews and without being circumcised), their way of life should also not break the Mosaic law—that is, not committing sexual immortality and keeping themselves from other impurities enjoined on all those who lived amid the people of God (15:20–21; cf. Lev. 17:8). Yet these were socially motivated directives since otherwise Gentile converts would not be able to interact with Jewish believers. The more important theological point was that following the Messiah did not result in disregard for the law but in experiencing the saving power of the law in the life of Jesus.

No wonder there was such opposition to Jesus and the apostolic leaders in Jerusalem initially and now to Paul and others who were taking the gospel to the Gentiles. The decision rendered by the apostles at this Jerusalem council was a radical one that in effect legitimized a non-Jewish form of messianic discipleship. Jews who were committed to the covenant promises could not easily find a way to remain faithful to their traditions while embracing the life and teachings of Jesus and his community simultaneously. In fact, it seemed as if God knew this would happen and that this rejection would itself be the occasion for the saving work of the Spirit among the Gentiles (13:46).

28
Parables of the Spirit's Work in the World

Luke 13:18-30; 15:1-32

IN LIGHT OF THE UNFOLDING OF THE STORY of Israel's restoration as including the Gentiles in Acts, the story of the prodigal son can be understood as anticipating the struggle of the elder brother, representing law-abiding Jewish followers of Jesus, to accept and receive the younger brother and profligate son, representing the God-fearers and Gentiles who were responding to the gospel. Note first that the younger brother goes off to a "distant country" (15:13), clearly indicative of Gentile territory (cf. Acts 22:21). After squandering his fortune, he resorts to working with swine (Lk. 15:15), which as anathema and impure to Jews (cf. Lev. 11:7) was a vocation undertaken only by Gentiles. Finally, he sacrilegiously wastes his inheritance "with prostitutes" (Lk. 15:30), often understood as referring to Gentile idolatry, and comes to realize that he is no longer a participant in the covenant God made with Israel (15:19).

The elder brother, however, had faithfully served his father and had kept the commandments (15:29). In some ways like the Jewish believers in Acts 15, he could not understand how to embrace his non-law-abiding prodigal brother (Gentiles). The father, who rejoiced at the homecoming of the prodigal—just as the shepherd did upon finding the lost sheep and the woman upon finding her lost coin—now enjoins the elder brother to be reconciled to the younger (15:32). If the elder brother in the parable was angry (15:28) and found it difficult to accept the transgressor as an equal family member, so also were the Jewish leaders incensed—to the point of persecuting and even murdering Stephen and James, and, so they thought, Paul—at the idea of Gentile followers of Jesus being entitled to the covenant promises. They could not fathom how uncircumcised sinners could merely by their repentance be equally chosen as the elect of God and as recipients of the blessings brought by the renewal of Israel.

Luke's portrait of the Jews is not easy to swallow at times. Even though the Jews appeared to have rejected the gospel and, through that, opened the door to the Gentiles, does that mean that God's covenant with the Jews has been revoked? The answer, drawing even from Luke's text, must be an emphatic no. James's citation of the prophet Amos at the Jerusalem council was,

> I will rebuild the dwelling of David, which has fallen;
>> from its ruins I will rebuild it,
>>> and I will set it up,
> so that all other peoples may seek the Lord.
> (Acts 15:16–17)

The Gentiles do not replace the Jews; rather, the Gentiles are enabled to enjoy repentance precisely because of the rebuilding of the house of David—the restoration and renewal and Israel.

The parable of the prodigal son thus show us God's great patience, persistence, and love for the lost, the marginalized, and, most importantly, the outcast and outsider. The time had come, with the sending of Jesus as the Christ, to renew the covenant with the Jews and, at the same time, to extend its benefits to the

Gentiles. This was the unbelievable work of the Spirit in these last days—to bring near the Gentiles who were once not only far off but also cut off from the promises of God, and to reconcile Jews and Gentiles so that they would be the one new people of God. Yet there was a danger for the Jews. As Paul had warned the Jews in Antioch in Pisidia: "It was necessary that the word of God should be spoken first to you. Since you reject it and judge yourselves to be unworthy of eternal life, we are now turning to the Gentiles" (Acts 13:46). In effect, the word of the kingdom and of eternal life was precisely that the restoration of Israel included the renewal of the world, so those Jews who rejected this message gradually found themselves being "left behind" while the Gentiles were caught up with the coming kingdom.

Jesus' own admonitions about these matters did not appear to have been heeded. At one point, he was asked a question debated among Jews of his time: whether or not there would be many or few who would inherit the kingdom and the covenant promises of God (Lk. 13:23). His response emphasized that his hearers should strive to receive salvation since it would not be accessible forever (13:24–25). Failure to repent now may lead to their exclusion from the great banquet later, and their places taken by the many who "will come from east and west, from north and south, and will eat in the kingdom of God" (13:29). So although the prophets had promised that the day of the restoration of Israel would also bring about blessings for all the peoples of the earth, Jesus was concerned that his hearers would finally miss out on the kingdom. The important question was not how many would be saved but how anyone could be saved. We can see how Paul's warning to his Jewish and Jewish Christian listeners was consistent with Jesus' own message and ministry.

But even amid the dire cautions we find reasons to be optimistic. While speaking in a synagogue on the Sabbath (Lk. 13:10), Jesus told two parables of the mustard seed and the leavened meal that indicated the coming of the all-inclusive (of Jews and Gentiles) kingdom, which was launched by seemingly insignificant events like the healing of a disabled woman (13:18–21). Just like the small mustard seed became a large tree for all the birds and just like the leaven spread throughout the entire meal, with the coming of Jesus and then the gift of the Holy Spirit, the invisible but no less active power of God was growing and cultivating the kingdom. The point is that as bleak as things might look, the kingdom is inexorably at work, accomplishing God's saving intentions.

So while we should not dismiss the warnings about being excluded from the coming kingdom, we should also not worry or be anxious about it. If God warned the Jews and also waits patiently for them, so also does God admonish all people to turn to him, even while waiting patiently for them. In fact, God so loves the world that he is seen to rejoice, along with the angels in heaven, over even one repentant sinner (15:7, 10). Is it any wonder then that God did not withhold himself, his very own Spirit, but instead poured out his Spirit on all flesh?

PART SEVEN

*The Holy Spirit Turns the World
Upside Down*

29
Your Daughters Shall Prophesy!

Acts 16:1-15; 21:7-11

E PICK UP THE APOSTOLIC STORY after the great Jerusalem council. The mission to the Gentiles had been affirmed, and Paul and his companions were now off to fulfill the task. Here in Acts 16, we see the Spirit at work in Paul in ways that display some of the themes Luke had specifically linked with the Spirit's outpouring on all flesh:

> Your sons and your daughters shall prophesy,
>   and your young men shall see visions,
>   and your old men shall dream dreams. (Acts 2:17)

The narratives regarding Timothy (16:1–5), Paul's vision (16:6–10), and Lydia (16:11–15) illustrate the ongoing work of the Spirit given for the sake of transforming the world.

Timothy was the son of a Greek father and a Jewish believer in the Messiah (16:1). Elsewhere we are told of the sincere faith of his mother and grandmother, Lois and Eunice (2 Tim. 1:5), and of how they had taught him, even from childhood, the sacred writings (2 Tim. 3:15). By the time of Paul's second journey to Derbe, Lystra, and Iconium, Timothy was already "well spoken of by the believers" (Acts 16:2) in that area. Having just lost Barnabas and Mark (15:38–40), Paul invited Timothy to continue with him on his mission through Asia Minor.

Timothy's life is exemplary of the work of the Spirit in various respects. First, his conversion and maturation as a follower of Jesus in such a short period of time is astonishing considering that just a few years ago the Jews in Timothy's hometown areas had run Paul out of Iconium and then stoned and left him for dead at Lystra (14:5–6, 19–20). Further, he embodied, biologically and culturally, the unity of Jew and Gentile made possible by the gift of the Spirit. Finally, his adult circumcision as a Jew was confirmation that the redemption of the Gentiles did not abrogate God's covenant with the Jews. Paul realized that his calling to the Gentiles did not mean the end of his mission to the Jews and that Timothy's reception in Jewish circles depended on his taking on the sign of the covenant (which was probably denied him as a child by his Greek father, who was now no longer alive). Timothy's circumcision did not undermine the decision of the Jerusalem council since that concerned Gentiles, and this was confirmed as Paul continued with him from town to town, delivering the council's letter to the churches (16:4–5).

While making their way through Galatia, Luke tells us that the Holy Spirit directed the apostolic crew by prohibiting their ministry in Asia and Bithynia (16:6–7). How this happened is unclear. Earlier in Acts, we see how the Holy Spirit launched the ministry to Samaria (through Philip and other Hellenistic Jewish deacons) in part by the severe persecution that broke out (8:1), even as later on, the Spirit directed Paul's first missionary journey in a more conventional manner, through congregational worship, fasting, and prayer (13:1–3). The means of the Spirit's leading during this second missionary journey is less clear, although at one point a vision is given, which Paul and his colleagues discern as leading them to Macedonia (16:9–10). As was promised by the prophet

Joel, the early Christians continued to follow the Spirit's leading through visions: here; earlier when Paul was on the Damascus road (9:10) and later when he was besieged by doubts at Corinth (18:9); and then also when Peter was led to Cornelius's house (10:3).

Does not the Holy Spirit still speak to the church through dreams and visions today? Many people are worried that reliance of such vehicles opens up to an unconstrained subjectivism and that people will get carried away believing they have heard this or that from God. In some, maybe even many, cases people are disillusioned. But our fears about dreams and visions have resulted in many of us ignoring them altogether. And when we do that, we close ourselves off to one of the modes through which God has perennially spoken. Of course, we should always judge and discern all dreams and visions, and such discernment occurs best in a community of faith.

The Acts 16 narrative also picks up on the theme about the outpouring of the Spirit on women (including younger women) for the renewal of Israel and the redemption of the world. Here Luke highlights the conversion of Lydia and her leadership in the evangelization of Philippi. There does not appear to have been a fully formed synagogue in this "leading city" (16:11) of Macedonia, but there were God-fearers whom Paul was able to find gathered from around the surrounding regions to seek God on the Sabbath. Lydia may have been wealthy since she appeared to have had a home large enough to host Paul and his team (which now included at least Timothy and probably Luke himself, as the "we" suggests in 16:11). Tabitha (see chapter 22 above) and Lydia provided matriarchal leadership in Joppa and the Philippi area respectively (cf. 16:40), and this during a time when patriarchal rule was normative.

Lydia and Tabitha are representatives of the Spirit's empowering the ministry of women in the early church. Other women we have already met in Acts include Mary the mother of Jesus and others in the upper room (1:14), Mary the mother of John Mark, and Rhoda, her servant (12:12–13). Women whom we have yet to meet include Priscilla the wife of Aquila and co-mentor of Apollos (18:2, 26); Damaris, a convert in Ephesus (17:34); other "leading women" converts in Thessalonica and Berea (17:4, 12); Paul's sister (23:16); and Queen Bernice (25:13).

Later, when Paul arrives in Caesarea to stay at the home of Philip the evangelist, we see ironically that Philip's evangelism to Samaria was previously initiated when Saul "was ravaging the church by entering house after house; dragging off both men and women" to prison (8:3)! We are told of his "four unmarried daughters who had the gift of prophecy" (21:9). These and many other unnamed women were recipients of the Spirit's gift and became prophesying maidservants of God, some literally (like Philip's daughters), but others simply by living out the mercifully inclusive character of the renewed Israel and the coming kingdom.

Yet it's also clear that despite the undeniable leadership roles played by Tabitha, Lydia, Philip's daughters, and others, women in Acts remain largely subordinated to men. Although Philip's daughters had the gift of prophecy, they are not even named, and the prophetic words in that passage come from Agabus instead (21:10–11). Lydia is said to have "prevailed upon" Paul and his coworkers, but her only recorded words are explicitly deferential to Paul's authority and judgment (16:15). In short, Joel's prophecy, as reiterated by Peter on the Day of Pentecost—that "your sons and your daughters shall prophesy"—appears to have been only partially fulfilled. Even in the twenty-first century we are still awaiting in many circles a more evident pentecostal outpouring that will enable women to fulfill their calling as prophesying daughters of the Spirit.

30
Jesus the Protofeminist! The Anointing of Women

Luke 8:1-3; 10:38-42; 24:1-12

HERE IS EVIDENCE IN JESUS' LIFE, ministry, and even teachings that he intended to initiate a radical and revolutionary understanding of women and their roles in the coming kingdom. Not only does Luke tell us about a good number of women in the gospel,[8] but also in many cases, these women's words and deeds challenge the social conventions for first-century Palestinian women. Jesus' ministry of proclaiming the kingdom of God was accompanied by men and women, and often provided for by the latter. Three women are prominent in Luke 8:1-3: Mary Magdalene, Joanna, and Susanna, although there were "many others" as well. They came from a diversity of backgrounds—Mary had previously been demon possessed, while Joanna was a woman of some means, being the wife of Chuza, Herod Antipas's steward. It is these women who were said to have "provided for them [not only Jesus but also the Twelve] out of their resources" (8:3). In so doing, these women were not only countering the patriarchalism of first-century patron-client relations but also anticipating the community of equals and of reciprocity formed out of the Pentecost event (Acts 2:44–47; 4:32–37).

Jesus' visit to the home of Mary and Martha showed that women were not confined to traditional female roles.[9] In this case,

Martha complained to Jesus that Mary was not helping her attend to the tasks of hosting Jesus, not to mention his followers who were accompanying him (Lk. 10:38). Yet while Mary "sat at the Lord's feet and listened to what he was saying" (10:39), Jesus affirmed her place among the disciples and rebuked Martha: "Mary has chosen the better part, which will not be taken away from her" (10:42).

The attention Mary and Martha give to Jesus is retained by the women followers of Jesus at and after his crucifixion, albeit in different ways. While there is every indication that the male disciples deserted Jesus during his hour of greatest need (see Matt. 26:56; Mk. 14:50), the women followed him—all the way from Galilee, it is noted—to his death (Lk. 23:49), observing where he was buried and making plans to return to anoint his body (23:55–56). They attended to Jesus' material needs not only in his life but also even after his death.

On the first day of the week, Mary Magdalene, Joanna, Mary the mother of James, and other women arrived to embalm Jesus' body but met instead two men who told them that Jesus had risen from the dead. At that moment "they remembered his words" (24:8), showing that unlike the men (but like Mary), they had not only heard Jesus' teachings but also kept his words in their hearts. These women became the first evangelists—the first to testify of the resurrected Christ—to the men who not only were despondent about the events of the previous week (cf. 24:17) but also dismissed the witness of the women as an "idle tale" (23:11). By proclaiming the risen Christ, these women, most of whom remain unnamed, were forerunners of the prophetic maidservants of the Spirit promised in Acts.

Jesus' attitude toward women indicates both that the redemption of Israel would turn the world upside down and that this included the rule of patriarchy. Thus there is a scandalousness, for instance, about Jesus' parable of the woman who lost her coin but goes out of her way to find it since the woman is analogous to the shepherd and God the Father in the surrounding parables (15:8–10). The idea that God could have been imagined in feminine terms and images would have been unthinkable according to the patriarchal conventions of this time. Through the overturning of patriarchy, what emerges is a new vision of male and female understood as equals in Christ (cf. Gal. 3:28).

The early messianists appeared to have understood this at least in terms of their expectation that the coming Spirit would empower not only men but also women (Acts 2:17–18). Yet, as we have seen, women still play a relatively minor role in Acts, nowhere approaching their significant contributions to the life and ministry of Jesus in the Gospels. So while the outpouring of the Spirit was supposed to have completed the radical revolution for women begun by Jesus, the inertia and forces of patriarchy appear to have regained the upper hand after the death of Jesus even among the disciples and have largely succeeded in maintaining the hierarchical division between male and female since.

What we need today is a "new Pentecost," a fresh outpouring of the Holy Spirit on all flesh, male and female, young and old. Males continue to need deliverance from their patriarchal mindset and practices, while women should discern the new thing that God seeks to do in and through their lives in restoring Israel and establishing the kingdom. The empowerment of women begun by the Spirit in Jesus and the early church continues to await completion and fulfillment.

31
Profit, Power, Politics, Praise

Acts 16:16-40

PAUL'S ENCOUNTER with the slave girl at Philippi has all of the elements fit for a tabloid. Here was a young woman whose powers of divination derived from the occultic arts (she is said to be possessed by a Pythian spirit—*pneuma pythona*; Acts 16:16—which refers to a mythical serpent or dragon that spoke then through a shrine at Delphi), whose fortune-telling was a source of great wealth to her owners, and who followed Paul and his associates around for days announcing, "These men are slaves of the Most High God, who proclaim to you a way of salvation" (16:17). Her announcement contained at least two half-truths: the reference to the "Most High God" would have been understood not monotheistically but polytheistically in Philippi, and the salvation the Pythonness spoke of was only one among others. (Notice the absence of the definite article before "salvation.") Finally, but apparently only after being exasperated beyond measure, Paul exorcised the Pythian spirit from the girl, and that in effect not only silenced her but also eliminated her powers of divination.

While we are left to wonder if the slave girl joined the messianic community, her owners were furious that their exploitative practices had come to a halt. So they dragged Paul and Silas before the local magistrates, saying, "These men are disturbing our city; they are Jews and are advocating customs that are not lawful for us as Romans to adopt or observe" (16:20–21). Not only do these charges reflect the xenophobia of the accusers, but the response of the crowd, amounting almost to a riot, also reveals the anti-Jewish ethos of the city. (Perhaps this is why the text does not indicate that Timothy, who was known to have a Gentile father, was detained, and it also clarifies why there was no synagogue in Philippi.) The city magistrates thus had them flogged, jailed, and maximally secured.

Confined, bleeding, and fearful about what the future held, Paul and Silas nevertheless resisted not according to the conventions of falsely accused imperial prisoners but according to the politics of the coming kingdom: with prayer, praise, and singing! And similar to when God sent an angel to release Peter from prison while the church was praying for him (12:5–11), so now God sends an earthquake that loosens the chains of all the prisoners in response to the prayers and praises of his servants. Clearly realizing the impending doom of the jailer—who, if he had not killed himself, would probably have had to pay with his own life for allowing the prisoners to escape—Paul somehow convinced the other prisoners to remain on the premises and assured the jailer: "We are all here" (16:28).

The jailer, perhaps having heard the Pythonness witness to the salvation of the Most High available through Paul and his comrades, asked: "What must I do to be saved?" (16:30). The response was, "Believe on the Lord Jesus, and you will be saved, you and your household" (16:31). He and his household believed and were saved—as were the households of Lydia (16:15), Cornelius (11:14), and, later, Crispus of Corinth (18:8)—with the firstfruits of his repentance being that he took them into his home and washed their wounds (16:33). That same night, the jailer and his household were all baptized, as was the practice since the Day of Pentecost (2:37–41), and the jailer may have joined with Lydia to become the founding members of the church at Philippi.

The next day, the oblivious magistrates ordered the police to release Paul and the others. Yet Paul insisted that the illegality of publicly beating a Roman citizen (himself) should not be covered up with a private dismissal. (There is no indication if Paul's attempt to communicate his status as a citizen the previous day was drowned out by the mob.) Having secured a public apology, Paul did not press countercharges in return—did he forgive his oppressors instead?—but proceeded on to the region of Thessalonica.

At one level, we can read this passage and conclude that the Holy Spirit is more powerful than the Python spirit; that the Holy Spirit inspires prayer and praise as the proper responses in our deepest and darkest hours of need; that the Holy Spirit is always at work, even through the most unexpected circumstances of our lives, to bring salvation to the lost. This is all right and true. In addition, however, we might observe the following insights into the presence and activity of the Spirit amid the pressures of imperial life:

- The Holy Spirit does not condone the exploitation of the poor (even those in servitude via use of the divining arts), especially by the wealthy;
- The practices of the kingdom, including praying and singing, are not only expressions of personal piety but are also public demonstrations of the Spirit's empowering followers of Jesus to be in but not of the world;
- The Spirit is interested not only in saving souls for eternity but in forming new communities of healing and reconciliation

from out of entire households that embrace the good news of Jesus and the kingdom.

Beyond this, we should notice that imperial citizenship provides another venue for the Holy Spirit's work of redeeming Israel and restoring the kingdom. Notice that Paul the Roman citizen responded in a manner that resulted not only in the literal salvation of the jailer from death but also in eternal life for him and his entire household; and Paul was then also able to confront the magistrates about their lack of oversight and perhaps even about the ethnocentricity and anti-Jewish sentiments that marked the Philippian community. In short, earthly citizenship brings with it not only rights but also responsibilities, and these, no less than praying and praising, are vehicles of the Spirit's work.

32
Praying for the Kingdom—Amid Empire

Luke 11:1-13; 18:1-8

*P*AUL AND SILAS were able to pray and praise even while in prison no doubt in part because they were simply following in the footsteps of Jesus and attempting to live out his teachings. The early Christians learned to view prayer as both a private but also public activity from the life and teachings of Jesus himself. We know that Jesus was a man of prayer, withdrawing often into the wilderness, either remaining there all night long or going out early before dawn to seek the will of the Father (Lk. 5:16; 6:12; 9:18, 28). Yet he also taught his disciples to pray as such:

> Father, hallowed be your name. Your kingdom come.
> Give us each day our daily bread.
> And forgive us our sins, for we ourselves forgive everyone
>   indebted to us.
> And do not bring us to the time of trial. (11:2–4)

Although most Christians have memorized Matthew's version of the prayer (Matt. 6:9–13), each of the four parts of Luke's rendition is consistent with the overall good news of Jesus' announcing the redemption of Israel and the coming kingdom. First, prayer should be addressed to our heavenly Father and reflect our discontent with the empires of this world and our yearning for the coming Day of the Lord. This is the "year of the Lord's favor" (Lk. 4:19) as well as the "great and glorious day" of the Lord, when "everyone [Jews and Gentiles] who calls on the name of the Lord shall be saved" (Acts 2:20–21).

Second, prayer emerges out of the concrete needs of our embodied and communal lives, which need daily sustenance. Thus, we ask for daily bread, and this God provides, whether miraculously through the multiplication of loaves and fishes (e.g., Lk. 9:13–17) or through the mutuality, generosity, and reciprocity of the apostolic community (Acts 2:44–47; 4:32–37). Here we cry for the economy of divine grace rather than for a temporary "fix it" of our market economy of exchange.

Third, prayer is about the forgiveness of sins and of debts, both our own and others'. From God we seek the forgiveness of sins; with regard to others, we forgive them the debts owed to us. This is consistent with the message of the divine forgiveness of sins proclaimed by Jesus and the apostles as well as with the Spirit-empowered ministry of Jesus to establish the Year of Jubilee, featuring the release of captives and those oppressed and the proclamation of the Day of the Lord to the poor (Lk. 4:18–19). The earliest followers of Jesus not only prayed about the forgiveness of sins and debts but also embodied its message through the selling of private property for the provision of the needs of the community.

Finally, prayer keeps us from trials and temptations and preserves us amid persecution (foretold by Jesus in 12:12–19 and experienced by his followers, such as Paul and Silas at Philippi). This reflects the interconnectedness of the vertical (our prayer addressed to the heavenly Father) and horizontal (public and political) dimensions of our lives. In each of these cases, the Lord's Prayer is not merely personal and individualized but also has to do with the public realm of the kingdom and hence interfaces with the political, economic, and social aspects of life in the here and now.

Jesus follows up his example of how or what to pray with a teaching about the Father, to whom we ought to pray. Two lessons are emphasized: first, if friends will share what they have in our times of need, then the Father in heaven will be much more willing to give when we ask and to open the door when we knock (Lk. 11:5–10); second, if human parents know how to give good gifts to their children—fishes instead of snakes, eggs instead of scorpions—"how much more will the heavenly Father give the Holy Spirit to those who ask him!" (11:13). The gift of the Spirit to all flesh reflects not just another good gift from God but is God himself, given for the renewal of Israel and for the salvation of the world.

Jesus also tells us, through the parable of the widow and the unjust judge (18:1–8), when to pray: always! The wider context of this parable concerns the coming of the kingdom (17:20–37). Perhaps by the time of Luke's writing, there were doubts about the imminent return of Jesus and the arrival of the kingdom (cf. 2 Pet. 3:3–13), and he therefore inserted this parable at this juncture, featuring Jesus' invitation "to pray always and not to lose heart" (18:1). This story of a widow, unjustly oppressed, may have been on the minds of Paul and Silas when they were shackled in their prison cell in Philippi, also unjustly thrashed and restrained. God's response to Paul and Silas was immediate, just as Jesus indicated the justice of God would not be delayed (18:7–8).

More importantly, the prayers of the righteous and oppressed are for justice—mentioned three times in the parable (18:3, 5, 7). Justice is promised by God in the restoration of Israel (against her enemies), as good news for the poor and the marginalized (against the rich aristocracy), and as liberation of the captives (from their oppressors). For the elect longing for the redemption of Israel, for liberation from captivity, and from the shackles of poverty, Jesus responds, "Will not God grant justice to his chosen ones who cry to him day and night?" (18:7). If human courts enforce the payment of debts (including those owed by widows to their creditors), then the Day of the Lord will bring about justice for all according to the merciful calculus of a gracious and gift-giving God.

So how then should we pray? Perhaps in the end the Spirit intercedes for us, within us, and through us in anticipation of the coming kingdom and the redemption of all creation (Rom. 8:19–27). We who long for the justice of God to be revealed only do so because the Spirit has already been poured out into our hearts as a down payment of the divine reign to come. Our prayers for peace and justice, then, constitute part of the Holy Spirit's work to establish shalom in the world today.

33
The Spirit Turns the World
Upside Down

Acts 17:1-18:21

E HAVE SEEN that the major theme of Luke's two-volume work, the redemption and renewal of Israel, is connected with the beginnings of the arrival of the kingdom and the gradual renewal of the world of the Gentiles. And we have seen that the Spirit's primary mode of accomplishing these objectives is to work in ways contrary to religious and social expectations: the poor are privileged, the rich demoted; the ruling classes are challenged to lead by servanthood, while the oppressed—women, ethnic minorities, and even people with disabilities—are central to the gospel narrative; and the religious leaders are somehow marginalized, while tax collectors, sinners, and Samaritans are included in the kingdom just as they are. In short, the pagan mob at Thessalonica was right when they said of Paul and his missionary workers: "These people who have been turning the world upside down have come here also" (Acts 17:6).

To be sure, the messianic mission had indeed "upset the apple cart" and caused a ruckus around the Mediterranean world. Yet another perspective would be to say instead that the Holy Spirit had turned the world right side up.

The good news of the kingdom both demanded a complete reversal of the world's values and arrived as a fulfillment of Jewish and Gentile hopes and aspirations. Both the discontinuity and the continuity can be seen throughout Paul's missionary endeavors at Thessalonica (17:1–9), Berea (17:10–14), Athens (17:15–34), and Corinth (18:1–18).

Beginning with the Jews, note again how the gospel stirred up hostile, even blasphemous, responses to the point that, in protest, Paul "shook the dust from his clothes and said to them: 'Your blood be on your own heads! I am innocent. From now on I will go to the Gentiles'" (18:6; which echoes Jesus' instructions to shake off one's foot dust before those who reject the gospel—cf. Lk. 9:5; 10:11). Jewish misconceptions continued regarding the way of the Messiah, as the Corinthian Jews persisted: "This man is persuading people to worship God in ways that are contrary to the law" (Acts 18:13). When they found their case against Paul summarily dismissed, they set instead on the leader of the synagogue, Sosthenes (18:17), perhaps a convert like the previous leader, Crispus (18:8), or perhaps someone who just had not quite come out in full support of the Jews in their charges against Paul.

There are also unmistakable continuities between the gospel and traditional Jewish beliefs and practices. Paul reasoned with the Jews from the Scriptures (17:2; 18:5), persuading some even while leading others to confirm what was said through the Jewish sacred texts (17:11). At Cenchrea, Paul fulfilled an earlier (probably Nazirite) vow and cut his hair (18:18),[10] even as he sought to attend the feast (of Passover) in Jerusalem (18:21). The decision of Gallio, the proconsul of Achaia, not to preside over intra-Jewish disputes (18:14–15) clarifies that even at this stage, the way of Jesus was still considered a sect within rather than wholly distinct from Jewish faith. In fact, Gallio's understanding of Christianity as just another Jewish sect is confirmed by the Emperor Claudius's decree from around 49 CE requiring all Jews to leave Rome (18:2) because of civil disturbances related to intra-Jewish disputes regarding Christ. In short, conversion to Jesus did not necessarily require rejection of Judaism.

Was this also the case for Gentiles? On the one hand, Paul's proclamation at the Areopagus—which may have been the cultural and philosophical capital of the ancient world—suggests not only that the Athenians worshiped the Creator of heaven and earth, albeit unknowingly (17:23–24) but also that the pagan poets testi-fied to this unknown God (17:28). Further, God's scattering of the Gentiles to their own dwelling places across the face of the earth was "so that they would search for God and perhaps grope for him and find him—though indeed he is not far from each one of us" (17:26–27). We had previously seen Paul approaching pagans by emphasizing God as Creator of the world (at Lystra; 14:15–17), which is consistent with Peter's declaration that "God shows no partiality, but in every nation anyone who fears him and does what is right is acceptable to him" (10:34–35). In short, one might view Gentile culture and even religiosity as anticipating fulfillment by the God revealed as the Father of Jesus Christ.

Paul also said: "While God has overlooked the times of human ignorance, now he commands all people everywhere to repent, because he has fixed a day on which he will have the world judged in righteousness by a man whom he has appointed, and of this he has given assurance to all by raising him from the dead" (17:30–31). Luke then notes that the mention of the resurrection—which remains central to the gospel message, whether for Jews or Gentiles (17:3, 18)—was not well received by the skeptical and rationalist Athenian philosophers (17:32). Last, there was the underlying claim regarding the kingship of Jesus (17:7), which, although not acted on in politically revolutionary ways by his followers, was nevertheless clearly subversive of both the religious symbolism and imperial authority of Caesar. In short, one might also view Gentile culture and religiosity not as being fulfilled by Christ but as being abrogated by the gospel.

The missionary ventures of Paul in these two chapters confirm that the gospel of Jesus Christ is both continuous with and yet also discontinuous from Jewish and Gentile culture and religiosity. The Spirit's redemption of culture requires a preservation of the old in some respects but also a repudiation of former beliefs and practices in other respects. If the work of the Spirit brought about a renewal, restoration, and reappropriation of all that was good and true in the social, cultural, and religious spheres of human life, it could also be seen from another perspective that the coming of the Spirit turned the world upside down in each of these domains of human endeavor. Continuity or discontinuity, when, and how? These are questions that require ongoing discernment of the Spirit's presence and activity.

34
The Spirit and the New World Dis/order

Luke 6:17-49

ROM THE TIME that they first began following Jesus, the disciples wrestled with the topsy-turvy world that Jesus had introduced them to. Soon after appointing them (Lk. 6:12–16), Jesus sat them down, along with a great crowd—mostly common people from the Judean countryside and the surrounding regions (6:17)—and taught them about the values of the kingdom. These blessings (of the poor, the hungry, those who weep now, and those who are hated by others for Jesus' sake) and woes (on the rich, the full, those who laugh now, and those who are spoken well of) reflect the reversals anticipated at the restoration of Israel (1:46–55). What the world values will be demoted and the opposite will be lifted up.

This reversal of values is not only something that will occur in the future, at the end of the world; but with the coming of Jesus, especially his resurrection and ascension, the "last days" had already begun (Acts 2:17). So these ideals of the kingdom were, beginning with Jesus, already operative. Thus, from Luke's perspective, the Good News belonged to the poor, the captives, the blind, and the oppressed now (4:18), not just later. So while Matthew's version of the beatitudes are spiritualized—"Blessed are the poor *in spirit*" and "Blessed are those who hunger and thirst *for righteousness*" (Matt. 5:3, 6, emphasis added)—Luke's focus was on the economically poor, the socially oppressed, the physically and materially disadvantaged, and the politically marginalized. These were the ones excluded by the present world order and who therefore would have been the most eager to depend not on conventional forms of power but on the surprising and unpredictable power of God.

What then would be the central manifestation of the divine power that would turn the world upside down and bring about the coming kingdom? While later Jesus would summarize the most important commandments as that of loving God and neighbor (Lk. 10:27), here he follows the blessings and curses by saying: "Love your enemies, do good to those who hate you, bless those who curse you, pray for those who abuse you. If anyone strikes you on the cheek, offer the other also; and from anyone who takes away your coat do not withhold even your shirt. Give to everyone who begs from you; and if anyone takes away your goods, do not ask for them again" (6:27–30). Jesus further clarifies that these practices of the kingdom represent additional contrasts to the way the world works. Even sinners (read: pagans and Gentiles) love those who love them, lend and give expecting something in return, and do good to those who do good in return to them. In short, the world works according to an economy of (even) exchange: people do to others as they expect others to do to them. So if followers of Jesus as the Messiah do to others expecting the same thing in return, they are acting no differently than the world.

However, God's economy of grace works differently. Thus Jesus said: "Love your enemies, do good, and lend, expecting nothing in return" (6:35). The earliest followers of Jesus not only recorded his words about loving their enemies (as in the parable of the good Samaritan) but also observed his loving response to those who put him to death. They emulated Jesus' life and teachings—as when Stephen forgave his opponents (Acts 7:60) and when Paul did not cease preaching the gospel to the Jews despite being stoned, jailed, and otherwise persecuted by his enemies.

Just as important, the early messianic believers embraced Jesus' kingdom values as well. The more affluent disciples sold what they had and gave to those in the peasant classes who had need (Acts 2:44–45 and 4:34–37). In response to those who persecuted them, such as the Hellenistic Jews (in Acts 6–7), the disciples took the good news of Jesus' forgiveness of sins into the wider Jewish Diaspora. Then the apostles also found themselves reconciled with the Samaritans, the despised enemies of the Jews. Even the wall between Jews and the (sinner) Gentiles was demolished by the gospel of the kingdom. If the world and its mechanisms emphasized a tit-for-tat economy of exchange in which one only did business with friends, patrons, clients, or those who could repay their efforts, the values of the kingdom proclaimed instead an economy of grace in which even enemies are transformed into family through the upside-down policies, structures, and relationships of the Spirit's work.

And Jesus recognized that, just as he himself was empowered by the Spirit, so also the Spirit's transformative work would be needed for his followers. How else would they be able to refrain from judging others or find it possible to forgive others (Lk. 6:37–38)? After all, not only are the blind unable to lead the blind; but also, left on our own as fallen, sinful, and hypocritical creatures, we are incapable of seeing through our log-jammed eyes so as to remove the specks in the eyes of our neighbors (6:39–42). Our human nature needs to be transformed and purified since only then can we produce good treasures out of our hearts and good words out of our mouths (6:43–45).

That is precisely what the gift of God himself, in the person of the Holy Spirit, accomplished on the Day of Pentecost. The reversed values of the kingdom would remain abstract teachings apart from the Spirit's transformation of the hearts, lives, and activities of the followers of Jesus; the practices of the kingdom would remain virtuous ideals apart from the Spirit's forming an alternative community and way of life; and the kingdom's economy of grace would remain only as a futuristic hope apart from the Spirit's making possible a new people of God who had "all things in common" (Acts 2:44). The pagan Thessalonians were right indeed—that the followers of Jesus had indeed "been turning the world upside down" (17:6)!

35

The Spirit and the Encounter of Money and Religion

Acts 19:18-41; 20:17-38; Luke 19:45-48; 20:20-26

F ON MARS HILL AND THE AREOPAGUS the Spirit challenged the conventions of the world through Paul's subversive use of the philosophical tradition, at Ephesus the Spirit turned the world upside down through subverting the local religious/pagan and political economy. The riot described in Acts 19 occurs at a major cultural and economic center, where the apostles were engaged with passionate devotees of the goddess Artemis (rather than engaging Athenian intellectuals merely at the level of ideas). Luke's report indicates the greatness of Artemis (the Greek name of the Latin goddess Diana)—that her majesty had "brought all Asia and the world to worship her" (19:27), that "the city of the Ephesians is the temple-keeper of the great Artemis and of the statue that fell from heaven" (19:35), and that "these things cannot be denied" (19:36). Worship of Artemis had been occurring in Ephesus for at least eight hundred years by this time (with some scholars suggesting an even earlier, eleventh-century-BCE origin of the cult in the city) and would persist at least until the fourth century CE. So great was the Artemis cult in this region that the temple devoted to the goddess was considered to be one of the seven wonders of the ancient world (alongside other monumental achievements like the great pyramid of Giza in Egypt and the hanging gardens of Babylon).

Interestingly, Paul remains in the background of the narrative rather than being prominently up front. We are told that among the friends who restrained him from attempting to respond to the mob were "some officials [literally "Asiarchs," high-ranking Roman administrators] of the province of Asia" (19:31), which suggests that Paul had successfully gained a hearing among the Ephesian elite during his two years of discussions in the hall of Tyrannus (19:8). Besides this dialogical approach to the Ephesian pagans, there are also other noticeable aspects to Paul's ministry in this renowned center of the ancient world. The most important is the witness of the city clerk who succeeded in dispersing the mob in part by reminding them that with regard to Paul and his compatriots, Gaius and Aristarchus (who had been detained by the crowd), "You have brought these men here who are neither temple-robbers nor blasphemers of our goddess" (19:37). So while Paul did contrast the living God with the lifeless idols made by artisan hands (19:26), the emphasis there seems to have been more on the incapacity of human craftsmanship to bear the majesty of deity than on being rudely dismissive. What is to be emphasized is that the Christian approach was not disrespectful of the religion of the Ephesians and that evangelism proceeded less by tearing down the faith of others than by bearing witness to Jesus Christ (19:17). This seems to be confirmed by Paul's own recollections that his ministerial attitude and practices were marked by humility, transparency (occurring not only in public but also from house to house), and a focus on God and the coming kingdom (20:19, 20, 25, 27).

It should not be overlooked that the disturbance that broke out at Ephesus was precipitated in large part by the impact of Christian evangelism on the religious economy of the area. Recall that mass conversions in the wake of the seven sons of Sceva incident (see chap. 25 above) had resulted in the burning of scrolls and other occultic paraphernalia amounting to "fifty thousand silver coins" (19:19). This led Demetrius and other leading silversmiths whose business was the production of shrines of Artemis to observe that the growth of the Way (of the Messiah) threatened their very economic livelihood (19:27).

Of course it was not only the cult of Artemis that fused cultural, religious, and economic matters. When Jesus entered the temple of Jerusalem, he "began to drive out those who were selling things there" (Lk. 19:45). How had the house of prayer become a "den of robbers" (19:46)? Two considerations deserve to be registered. First, because the temple had become an international center for the Jewish Diaspora of the first century, it provided a currency exchange system so that the many visitors could purchase the sacrificial animals needed to observe Jewish religious rites and festive celebrations. Second, the Jewish religious and cultural leadership in Palestine managed to keep the temple open and operative in part by agreeing to collect and pay a temple tax to the Roman authorities. This was justified as a legitimate compromise in order to either avoid the closure of the temple or ceding of local control of the temple to the Roman hierarchy.

Jesus' cleansing of the temple was indicative of the fact that practical exigencies had devolved over time into the corruption of religious rites by economic greed. Perhaps his driving out those buying and selling, as well as the money changers and merchandisers (mentioned in Mk. 11:15–16), amounted to an exorcism that sought to make possible again the kind of authentic religious prayer that would enable discernment of the time of divine visitation on the city and the people (Lk. 19:44). Yet in none of the other parallel Gospel accounts of this event is anything said about those who collected the temple tax. When asked about the payment of taxes in the hopes of ensnaring Jesus as an insurrectionist, Jesus noted that the coin bore the image of the emperor—to be more specific, the Roman denarius would have read: "Tiberius Caesar, Son of the Divine Augustus"—and then responded: "Give to the emperor the things that are the emperor's, and to God the things that are God's" (20:25). For his Jewish hearers, the mandate was unmistakable: the political authority whose image was stamped on the coin was to be honored through the payment of taxes. (Note that in 2:1–5 Luke does not chide Joseph and Mary for proceeding to register in their hometown, a political process directly related to Rome's taxation policies.) But the divine authority whose image was stamped on their lives (created as they were in God's image) was to be honored through the presentation of their very bodies "as a living sacrifice, holy and acceptable to God, which is your spiritual worship" (Rom. 12:1).

The events at Ephesus invite us to think further about both the contemporary Christian encounter with other religions and the complex interrelationship between religion and economics. It is worth noting that at times the evangelistic zeal displayed by Paul, who wanted to address the crowd and defend his coworkers against the riotous Ephesians, should sometimes be tempered by a patient, nonprovocative, and deferential posture. When we are guests of those in other faiths, proper protocols may dictate courses of action that are reverent and courteous rather than aggressive or confrontational. Just as important is the recommendation of the town clerk that any interreligious tensions should be resolved through the right judicial channels.

The interconnections between religion and economics are no less palpable today than they were at Ephesus and Jerusalem two thousand years ago. Most religious institutions are tax exempted, which raises all kinds of complex questions about the church-state relationship, even while there is a consumerist mentality for religious products such as Christian music, books, movies, and so on that are "big business" in the global market. In short, might our faith today be even more compromised by the capitalist system than was the cult of Artemis or the Jewish temple economy of the first century?

In this context, the words of Saint Paul are worth recalling— "I coveted no one's silver or gold or clothing" (Acts 20:33)—even as Paul's quotation of the words of Jesus are to be embraced and emulated: "It is more blessed to give than to receive" (20:35). Both point the way forward to how we might keep our religious faith free from economic contamination. More importantly, both lived out the gracious, abundant, and overflowing hospitality of God, who poured out his Spirit on all flesh so that it might be possible for us to participate in and extend God's gift of himself, the never-ending, always perpetuating, and continually multiplying salvation meant for the redemption of Israel and the renewal of the world. In fact, Christian ways of life that reflect these values would be subversive in our time of the religious and political economies of our world, and our persistent practices of Jesus' ethic would indeed turn upside down the conventions of our contemporary economic practices.

PART EIGHT

Toward the Ends of the Earth

36
The Spirit as Witness to the Resurrection

Acts 21:1-26:32; Luke 12:1-12

PAUL PERSISTED IN VISITING JERUSALEM in spite of the warnings he'd received along the way about the persecution he would suffer there. The Holy Spirit had warned Paul about imprisonments and hardships (Acts 20:22–23; 21:4), and the prophet Agabus had even enacted Paul's binding and handing over into Gentile custody (21:10–11). Nevertheless, Paul returned to Jerusalem, and when he arrived, he was informed that the thousands of believing Jews, in their zeal for the law (21:20), were concerned about what they had heard—that Paul had led many to apostasy. Paul agreed to join four brothers in their temple rite of purification and pay their expenses in order to demonstrate his Jewish commitments to the law.

However, Jews from Asia (21:27; cf. 24:19) came upon the temple, assumed that Paul's Gentile companions had entered into the sacred space with him (thus defiling the temple), and led a mob to seize Paul. In his defense before that crowd (22:2–21), Paul emphasizes his Jewish credentials: fluency in Aramaic, the daily language of the Jews; trained under Gamaliel, the leading Pharisee; zealous for the law; a follower of a Jewish Nazarene; assisted by Ananias, "who was a devout man according to the law and well spoken of by all the Jews living there" (22:12); appointed by the God of the Jewish ancestors; and devout in temple piety. But when the crowd hears that Paul understands his calling as a witness to the Gentiles, they reject his testimony and seek to kill him.

The Roman commander, Claudius Lysius, who was charged with keeping the peace in the city, takes Paul into custody quickly. Acts 23–26 records Paul's self-defenses in the presence of Claudius Lysius (along with the Sanhedrin, who had been assembled), Felix the governor of Judea and his successor Festus, and King Agrippa II. While the commander was concerned with the intensifying pro-Jewish and anti-Roman sentiments in the region (remember, this was probably no more than ten years before the Jewish rebellion in 66 CE), Felix was hoping for a bribe from Paul in exchange for his freedom, and both Felix and Festus sought to ingratiate themselves with the Jews (24:26–27). However, none could find fault with Paul, and he was declared innocent four times: by Claudius, Festus, and Agrippa (23:29; 25:18; 26:31–32), not to mention by the Pharisees as well (23:9), a sequence of events perhaps intended by Luke to parallel the repeated pronouncements of Jesus' innocence.

Of course, the Jewish leaders formally charge Paul not only with desecrating the temple but also with being "a pestilent fellow, an agitator among all the Jews throughout the world, and a ringleader of the sect of the Nazarenes" (24:5). To be sure, Paul's message had stirred up Jewish crowds all over the Mediterranean world. But why?

"I am on trial concerning the hope of the resurrection of the dead" (23:6), Paul declares at one point before the Sanhedrin, which was composed of conservative Sadducees (Torah legalists that did not believe in the resurrection because it was not in the first five books of the Bible; cf. Lk. 20:27) and the more-progressive Pharisees (who accepted the resurrection from other biblical passages). Paul would reiterate this claim, driving home both the point that the hope of the resurrection was anticipated by most Jews based on the covenant promises made to their ancestors and that this hope had come to fulfillment in Jesus.

But why would Paul's declaration that the hope of Israel culminated in Jesus of Nazareth have caused such consternation among his fellow Jews? The issue was that if Jesus had risen from the dead, then not only was he the promised Messiah, but the end of the age had also come (see 2:17). A risen Messiah meant also both that the renewal of Israel was at hand and that, as promised to Abraham (Gen. 12:3) and reiterated by the prophets, such restoration included Israel as being a blessing to the Gentiles. If the resurrection of Jesus had occurred, then that happened by the power of the Holy Spirit, and the same power of the Spirit was present to bring about a fulfillment of the covenant promises, even to the ends of the earth. Thus did Paul continue to link the hope of Israel and the resurrection with his being sent to proclaim the gospel to the Gentiles.[11] Resurrection meant good news not only for individual persons and dead/buried bodies but also for human community: sins would be forgiven and people would be reconciled to one another. As Paul clarified elsewhere, Jesus' death and resurrection meant the creation of a new people of God consisting of Jews and Gentiles (Eph. 2:11–22). Paul was persecuted by his fellow Jews because he not only believed in the hope of Israel but also sought to realize the full scope of the covenant promises among the Gentiles. Jesus had himself promised his followers that they would be persecuted and that some of them would even be granted the opportunity to bear witness to the gospel before kings and governors (Lk. 21:12). But he had also encouraged them to be courageous about their testimony: "When they bring you before the synagogues, the rulers, and the authorities, do not worry about how you are to defend yourselves or what you are to say; for the Holy Spirit will teach you at that very hour what you ought to say" (12:11–12).

Luke's account of Paul's witness even while in chains reflects the ongoing empowerment of the Holy Spirit in the direst of circumstances. This was a fulfillment of what the Spirit poured out on all flesh would accomplish (Acts 2:17–18): the empowerment of menservants and maidservants—literally slaves and those imprisoned—to prophesy in the name of the Lord. The gift of the Spirit was to enable the taking of the gospel beyond Judea and Samaria "to the [Gentiles at the] ends of the earth" (1:8). Paul's imprisonment would not hinder his eventual arrival at Rome, the symbolic center of the world of the Gentiles; in fact, it was precisely the unfolding events of his captivity that led to his appeal to Caesar and his journey to Rome. Thus, Paul's readiness to testify about Jesus, even to the point of death (25:11), and his success in doing so, remains the central theme of this last quarter of the book of Acts.[12]

Even today, Paul's own "passion" experience can be a model for us. What is impossible on our own strength can be accomplished by the power of the Holy Spirit. When we are persecuted for our faith, the Spirit will nevertheless empower our witness; then, even if our testimony is rejected, we are planting the seeds of the gospel that will germinate in the redemption of Israel and the salvation of the world. In the end, then, our story is not ours alone; rather, it is our participation through the Spirit in the story of Jesus' coming to save the world, as foretold to Abraham and proclaimed by the prophets of old.

37
Nature and the Cosmic Spirit

Acts 27:1-44; Luke 8:22-26

ECALL PETER'S EXPLANATION, from the Day of Pentecost, when he drew upon the prophet Joel in order to mention how the outpouring of the Spirit would be connected with incidents in the heavens and the earth:

And I will show portents in the heaven above
> and signs on the earth below,
>> blood, and fire, and smoky mist.
The sun shall be turned to darkness
> and the moon to blood,
>> before the coming of the Lord's great and glorious day.
(Acts 2:19–20)

This apocalyptic language highlights the cosmic transformation associated with the passing away of one era and the arrival of the new eon of the Spirit. If in the old dispensation the sun, moon, and seas were sometimes thought to be fatefully aligned with unfriendly astronomical powers, then the new age of the Day of the Lord would feature the redemption of these creations once called "good." The sun will give forth the light of God himself, the moon's brilliance will reflect the divine light, and the waters of the sea will once again nourish earthly life. If in the former epoch the "laws of nature" prevented a successful catch of fish all night long, the Day of the Lord would bring about a transfiguration of nature's rhythms so that the morning after, these same fisherman "caught so many fish that their nets were beginning to break" (Lk. 5:6). Similarly, if in the previous age earthquakes were feared as vengeful acts of the gods, after the outpouring of the Spirit, earthquakes would bring about a release of believers in prison instead (Acts 16:26). In short, nature's destructiveness will have been overcome and even redeemed so that the salvation of God could be made manifest in and through nature's movements.

Now, consider the apostle Paul in Acts 27. Paul's appeal to Caesar eventually lands him and his compatriots on a sea voyage toward Rome under the custody of Julius, "a centurion of the Augustan Cohort" (27:1). This sea narrative corresponds well with the shipwreck epics in the Greco-Roman literary tradition. Yet throughout, Paul the holy man remains the central character. Midway through, the journey is punctured by Paul's ominous admonition—which went unheeded—about the loss of the cargo, the ship itself, and even of many lives (27:10). Then, after days of listing through and being battered by the predicted storm and after suffering loss of cargo and the ship's tackle, Paul reemerges with a word of exhortation and comfort, in effect saying that, although the sailors had ignored his warning, God has unfinished business for Paul and thus none would suffer the loss of life. This encouragement was mediated by an angel, whose authority the pagan sailors would have recognized even if they may not have understood references to either Yahweh or the God of Jesus Christ.

If Paul is the main character, God's saving power (*soteria*, which is the root word for the English soteriology—the doctrine of salvation) is the fundamental theme of this sequence of events. Within the bigger picture of Luke, God's salvation was required in order to ensure Paul's safe arrival in Rome, to bear witness to Caesar (27:24; cf. 19:21; 23:11). Yet on the way to Rome, the salvation of God is expressed through Paul to the pagans. Luke notes amid the pounding of the tempest on the ship that they "had been without food for a long time" (27:21), and eventually, "all hope of our being saved was at last abandoned" (27:20). It was during this time of utmost desolation that the promise of God came: "There will be no loss of life among you, but only of the ship" (27:22). Later, after more than two weeks at sea and sensing land not too far ahead, some of the sailors thought about escaping from the ship on a lifeboat; however, Paul warned, "Unless these men stay in the ship, you cannot be saved" (27:31). That same morning, he urged, "Therefore I urge you to take some food, for it will help you survive [sōtērias]; for none of you will lose a hair from your heads" (27:34). In the end, Luke reports God as being true to his promise: "So it was that all were brought safely [diasōthēnal] to land" (27:44).

Part of the theological message communicated through this tale concerns divine power over the elements of the cosmos. In the ancient world, it was thought that the forces controlling the seas belonged to the gods (at best) or other hostile spiritual beings (at worst). So when Jesus and the disciples' lives were endangered by the storm while crossing the lake, Jesus "woke up and rebuked the wind and the raging waves" (Lk. 8:24). The word describing Jesus' taking authority over the squall, epetimēsen ("rebuke"), is the same word used earlier in the Gospel to depict how Jesus confronted the demoniac in the synagogue at Capernaum (4:35). The demon was exorcised in the synagogue while, on the lake, Jesus overcame the power of chaos as the winds and waves "ceased, and there was a calm" at his command (8:24). Thus Jesus the Christ, the one anointed by the Holy Spirit, reveals the power of God to tame even the destructive forces of nature. Though no immediate stilling of the storm occurred for Paul, the salvific power of God was no less present to all on that fateful trip.

Thus we see the healing and life-giving power of nature's gifts registered even in the midst of the shipwreck. After two weeks despairing against the winds and the waves, Paul urged the 276 on board to eat: "Then all of them were encouraged and took food for themselves" (27:36). The God who saved the entire crew and passengers (prisoners as well) from out of the storm showed himself as the "God who made the world and everything in it" (17:24), including the food that nourishes those who had despaired of their very lives. Paul was not conducting a Eucharistic celebration, even if many of the elements of the sacramental rite were present. Yet the taking of food involves consuming the goodness of creation and receiving through nature's endowments the saving power of the Spirit of God.

38
The Spirit and the Eucharist

Luke 9:10-17; 22:14-23; 24:13-35

T DAWN ON THE DAY of their shipwreck, Paul "took bread; and giving thanks to God in the presence of all, he broke it and began to eat" (Acts 27:35). This is a fairly traditional rite of prayer that would have been performed before meals by all pious Jews. At the same time, the ritual here recalls the mealtime actions of Jesus in the Gospels. On three other occasions—the feeding of the five thousand, the Last Supper, and on the road to Emmaus—we are told that Jesus also took bread, blessed or gave thanks for it, broke it, and gave it to others (Lk. 9:16; 22:19; 24:30). The bread on the ship was a sign of hope and salvation, as the bread in the Gospels was itself a symbol of the hope and life available through Jesus.

To understand the significance of the bread as a life-giving reality on the road to Emmaus, we need to follow the disciples' experiences on that journey. The two disciples on the way to Emmaus were clearly despondent in light of the death of Jesus (24:17–21). And while Jesus instructed them from the Scriptures on their walk, they did not perceive his presence until he sat down to eat with them. Although a guest in their midst, Jesus played the host in leading them in the prayer of blessing over the meal. They told the other disciples about how Jesus "had been made known to them in the breaking of the bread" (24:35). The living presence of Jesus had energized and emboldened them with hope.

At the Passover table, Jesus had already stated that his life and body would be represented by the cup and the bread, the meal's central elements. After he had taken a loaf, given thanks, and broken and distributed it, he said: "This is my body, which is given for you. Do this in remembrance of me" (22:19). There are a number of aspects to how a Christian celebration of this meal enables a remembrance of Jesus. First, the broken bread and poured-out cup are symbols of Jesus' wounded body and spilled blood and serve as a reminder of his having given his life as a seal of the new covenant and a down payment in anticipation of the kingdom of God (22:18, 20). Second, to "re-member" would also suggest that the celebration of the meal by the followers of Jesus would in effect reconstitute the members of his broken body. The result would be that the Jesus who is remembered would also be the Jesus who is present in the midst of those who celebrate the pouring out of his life for others.

Yet the feeding of the five thousand men, plus women and children, anticipates that Jesus' giving of himself to others is but a model for his followers. While the miraculous nature of the feeding should not be downplayed, Jesus' blessing, breaking, and giving of the bread and fish is but part of the larger sequence of events in which his disciples are involved in serving the crowd. The disciples had initially asked Jesus to send the crowd away, perhaps back to the city of Bethsaida (9:10), to find lodging and nourishment. But as Jesus had specifically told them to take neither food nor money on their mission (9:3), so now he enacted the provision of God and involved the disciples. They were told to organize the crowd, then released to serve them, and finally gathered up the leftovers (9:14–17).

The feeding of this large number of people reveals the all-inclusive table that Jesus spread before the crowd. Whereas Jewish purity laws would have been concerned about eating with the impure (for whatever reason), there is no concern relayed in the text that either Jesus or his disciples were worried about eating with the unclean and with women (who often ate separately in public meal events). This reflects Jesus' meal-eating habits as relayed in the rest of the Gospel narrative. Jesus ate not only with his disciples and the Pharisees but also with tax collectors and sinners. More importantly, Jesus' open table anticipated the final and great banquet of the kingdom, which he expected to celebrate with both his disciples (22:15) and the poor, crippled, blind, and lame (14:13, 21). In other words, while Jesus ate the final Passover only with the twelve apostles (which included among them Judas his betrayer), he also modeled inclusive eating practices that embraced those who otherwise might not have been invited for a meal.

We can see that the earliest followers of Jesus continued his practices of open fellowship. They continued to break bread together, remembering Jesus in the process (Acts 2:42, 46; 20:7). That the table of the Lord was to be open to even the Gentiles was confirmed in a vision to Peter, which led him to enter Cornelius's home and eat with him (10:48). Thus was Paul himself, an apostle to the Gentiles, comfortable with breaking bread and eating with the pagans on that fateful voyage.

Yet the redemptive power symbolized in eating together is further intensified when we consider that the cup and the bread celebrated the broken, life-giving body of Jesus poured out for the sake of the world. Thus the open table is an occasion not only for remembering Jesus' death but also reenacting a life lived for others. The meal is possible because of the service that makes possible the eating together. As the disciples served the crowds in the countryside, so also did they serve those from the Diaspora gathered in Jerusalem after the Day of Pentecost, and so also did other leaders like the Hellenistic Jewish deacons (6:3–6) serve the large population of widows and others who were most vulnerable within the fledgling community.

The breaking of bread together was a high point made possible by the acts of service before and after the meal, performed by those who were committed to following in the footsteps of Jesus, who gave himself fully to others in the power of the Spirit. And the same Spirit continues to be present and active among believers in Jesus, making him present and enabling recognition of him on each occasion that his supper is celebrated, empowering the life-giving service that nourishes the community of faith and renewal of the world and providing the hope of his resurrection life to all who are in despair and in need of salvation. This happened in and through Paul, in a boatload of pagans, and it will continue to happen to the ends of the earth if we are open to being conduits of the Spirit, who has been poured out on all flesh.

39
Barbarians, Believers, and the Spirit of Hospitality

Acts 28:1-31

THE SHIPWRECK LEFT THE SEAFARERS STRANDED on the island of Malta. The islanders—literally *barbaroi*, transliterated as "barbarians" (Acts 28:2, 4), which was used with reference to those who knew neither Greek culture nor its language—not only welcomed them but over the next three months also showed them kindness, entertained them with hospitality, and provided them with provisions for the next leg of their journey. Part of this was motivated by their realization of a holy man in their midst, one who withstood a snakebite (which protection was promised by Jesus—cf. Lk. 10:19; Mk. 16:18) and then who healed, through prayer, the sick father of Publius, the island's leading official, and others who were sick.

Yet, strangely, there is mention neither of Paul's preaching to the natives nor of any conversions among them. Perhaps because of the language barriers (although it is possible that the Maltese were fluent in the Punic dialect, which may have been related to Phoenician and, through that, to the Aramaic that Paul spoke), the followers of Jesus may have been unsuccessful in communicating the gospel. Yet, as Jesus has already said, "Whoever listens to you listens to me, and whoever rejects you rejects me, and whoever rejects me rejects the one who sent me" (Lk. 10:16), so it seemed clear that these pagan barbarians had, by showing generosity and hospitality to Paul and his compatriots, also received his Lord and Savior as their own (cf. Matt. 25:35–40).

Is it possible that we might learn a few important lessons from Paul's interactions with the barbarous Maltese islanders? Christians, especially those who have a missionary heart for evangelization, often think of themselves as bearers of the Good News and thus as hosts of a needy world. In this case, however, it is Paul who is the needy one and is the guest of unbelievers. While it is important to develop a theology of hospitality that underwrites how followers of Jesus should be welcoming to nonbelievers, it is also essential that we give more thought to developing a theology of guests that enables us to receive the hospitality of strangers and people of other faiths. This will enable us to be givers as well as receivers. Along the way, we might learn to appreciate that our bearing witness through the power of the Spirit involves not only our speaking about the things of the gospel but also receiving the hospitality of others. In short, our testimony is borne not only in what we say but also perhaps more importantly in how we live, how we interact with others, and how we are able to receive of the gifts of others as well.

Over the course of his story, Luke had actually told of Jesus' restoring the kingdom to Israel, except that it had begun to happen in a way that was completely unexpected to most of the Jews. Whereas Jews had the hope that the Messiah would deliver them from the hands of the Romans and restore the land and temple to them, for Paul, the "hope of Israel" (28:20) had to do with the resurrection of Jesus, the dawning of the kingdom, and the beginning of the new age in which the renewal of Israel would include the salvation of the Gentiles as well. Insofar as the Jews resisted the extension of the God's saving mercies to the Gentiles, to that same degree they also rejected the messengers—the apostles, including Paul—who attempted to persuade them otherwise. So while Paul maintained this witness with steadfastness, persisting even long after he had arrived at Rome, where he continued to entertain guests during his house arrest, the results were mixed. On the one hand, some believed (28:14), but on the other, the stubbornness of the Jews led Paul to proclaim "that this salvation of God has been sent to the Gentiles; they will listen" (Acts 28:28).[13]

In the meanwhile, the lives of those following after Jesus as Messiah will continue to stir up discussion, as the Jews in Rome said: "With regard to this sect we know that everywhere it is spoken against" (Acts 28:22). Yet such a ruckus will not be because Christians have been breaking the law, as Paul had been repeatedly cleared of any wrongdoing. Instead, the consternation will continue since any talk about a coming kingdom of God and any attempts to live out the way of the kingdom will inevitably conflict with the imperial aims of worldly kingdoms—and when such happens, the violence that marks fallen humanity will once again rear its ugly head.

Even when this happens, the Spirit, who has been poured out on all flesh, will continue to inspire and empower the peaceable, healing, and reconciling works of Jesus in order to enact the kingdom of God in the hearts and lives of human beings. The Spirit's raising Jesus from the dead was the first act of God's vindicating the righteous and setting into motion what would eventuate in the kingdom, and this has been followed by Jesus' pouring out of this same Spirit onto all—Jew and Gentile—for the sake of the salvation of the world. Luke does not tell us what happened with Paul, but he clearly informs us that Paul never ceased "proclaiming the kingdom of God and teaching about the Lord Jesus Christ with all boldness and without hindrance" (28:31). He simply continued to live by the power of the Spirit as a witness to the living Christ. The next chapters of the book of Acts, if they were ever to be written, would tell more about men and women, even perhaps among us today, who are also empowered by the Spirit of God to proclaim and enact the kingdom of God to the ends of the earth.

Epilogue

*T*HE BOOK OF ACTS ends without providing any closure regarding Paul's captivity. Some speculate that Luke completed his book while Paul was still imprisoned, while others believe that Luke finished his account with the arrival of the gospel at Rome and thus did not feel the need to provide any details about Paul's trial before Caesar. Still others are divided between those who think Paul was martyred by Emperor Nero or that he was released and undertook his long-anticipated mission to Spain.

For our purposes, the open-endedness of Acts 28 suggests that the work of the Holy Spirit begun in the life of Jesus and among the early church continues to the present. The emphasis throughout this book, however, has been to explore not just the private aspects of the Spirit's work in the hearts of believers in Jesus but also the public dimensions of the Spirit's activities in the political, economic, and social domains of the Roman Empire during the first century CE. We have seen that the redemption of Israel and the salvation of the world were being accomplished amid the concrete imperial forces of the Pax Romana and that the power of God was manifest in, through, and against the principalities and powers in these realms.

There is no reason to believe that the workings of the Holy Spirit in the first century have ceased or taken any different form since. The power of the Spirit at work in the public square, then, has been no less available to followers of Jesus the Messiah during the intervening two thousand years and is certainly present to all today. Living out the ways of the kingdom in our time is as challenging now as it was for the earliest disciples, especially in light of our political regimes of corruption, anarchy, tyranny, and environmental neglect, among other challenges; our economic systems of globalization, consumerism, and exploitative capitalism, among other unjust practices; and our social conventions that perpetuate racism, sexism, and able-ism, among other discriminatory regimes. Yet we should be inspired to know that the same Spirit who empowered Jesus and the early Christians to confront the principalities and powers of their day is the same Spirit who remains God's gift to empower all flesh today.

This does not mean that we hop on any political, economic, or social bandwagon in order to "engage the issues." It means that we are supposed to live faithfully with others who are seeking to follow Jesus so that we can be nurtured in the virtuous practices that the Spirit will use in our relationships with the world. It means that we need to continue to discern how the Spirit might inspire the church toward an ongoing faithfulness in a pluralistic and complex world.

The worst-case scenario is that our witness to Christ will end up in martyrdom, but even if so, such will be enabled by the power of the Spirit. At the least, we will continue to be persecuted, if for no other reason than that our witness presents a stark contrast to the world, much like the early followers of the Messiah were accused of being "sectarian" (or "heretical," from *haireseōs*—Acts 24:5; 24:14; 26:5; 28:22). These are manifestations of the Spirit's power that enable us to call into question the status quo and conventions of the societies in which we live, to resist the politics of conformity that are imposed upon us, and to develop alternative forms of exchange that expose the violence underlying the economies of this world.

At the very least, as our walk with the apostles through the book of Acts, with regular glances backward to the Third Gospel, has shown, we will continue to be surprised by how the Spirit works in our hearts to change the world. Along the way, we will have the memory of Jesus to guide us and his presence in the power of the Holy Spirit to inspire us. And the Spirit who has indeed been poured out upon all flesh will continue to do through us what was done through the apostles—turn the world upside down—if we would indeed be open and obedient to the Spirit's promptings. And it is only as we follow the winds of the Spirit in these acts of witness that we will continue to participate in the work of Jesus to renew Israel and, through that, to redeem and save the world. Toward this end, our prayer can only be, "Come Lord Jesus," while we continuously wait for and discern the fresh winds of his Spirit in the world.

Leaders' Study Guide and Small Group Discussion Questions

*R*ECOMMENDATIONS: Have group members read the chapter ahead of time and bring their Bibles to the discussion. Throughout the study, remember that references to "the public" or "the political" involve all aspects of our lives, including our economic, social, civic, political, and spiritual decisions and actions.

INTRODUCTION

What are the highlights of the books of Luke and Acts that you are familiar with, and why do these stand out in your mind? What else might you be looking forward to in reading and studying these books this time?

Do you agree with the author's suggestion that the work of the Holy Spirit not only pertains to individual hearts and lives but also has a more public and political significance? Why or why not?

Luke-Acts unfolds during the "Peace of Rome," in the days of Caesar. Can you anticipate what Luke will say or what you hope to read about with regard to the public or political implications of the life of Christ and of the experiences of the earliest followers of Jesus?

CHAPTER 1

How does it feel to read Luke-Acts "backwards" (starting in Acts and going back to Luke as appropriate)? Discuss the reason for this strategy of reading given by the author (see p. xiii) and how it works for illuminating the section on the election of Matthias.

What were the disciples expecting regarding the restoration of the kingdom to Israel (Acts 1:6)? If you had been a Jewish follower of Jesus in those days, would you have been expecting anything different from what the disciples expected or from what actually happened?

The disciples lived under the shadow of imperial Rome during the first century; do we live amidst an imperialism or in another kind of modern Western empire today? What are the prospects for a Spirit-filled Christianity under these conditions?

CHAPTER 2

Review Mary's song—historically known as the Magnificat—in Luke 1:46–55 and discuss how it interfaces with the public or political reading of Luke-Acts we are undertaking.

What did "the consolation of Israel" (Simeon in Luke 2:25) and "the redemption of Jerusalem" (Anna in Luke 2:38) mean to first-century Jews? What should they mean for us today?

How did Jesus challenge the lordship of Caesar back then? How is Jesus' lordship a challenge even for Spirit-filled Christians today?

CHAPTER 3

Why are the geographic references in the Pentecost narrative important?

Are prophesying daughters and young men seeing visions important for the life of the church today? Why or why not?

The word "upon my slaves" can also be translated "upon my servants"—what is the significance of this difference in translation in the two-thousand-year history of Christianity and today?

CHAPTER 4

What are the public aspects of the Davidic or messianic figure, and how does Peter's sermon highlight Jesus' fulfillment of those charismatic designs?

What specific sin did the crowd realize they needed to repent for, a sin that Peter promised would be forgiven (hint: see Acts 2:23 and 36)? How do you think Peter's message would have hit you if you had been in the crowd on that Day of Pentecost?

Are there public dimensions of the forgiveness of sins today? Why or why not?

CHAPTER 5

What were the consequences of repentance in the message of John the Baptist? How would such preaching and its effects come off (or not) in today's world?

What were the consequences of repentance for Zacchaeus? What would be the aftereffects of such actions in today's world?

Why have we by and large spiritualized and individualized the message of repentance and forgiveness? What, if anything, about these tendencies do even Spirit-filled Christians need to change?

CHAPTER 6

Acts 2:41–47 has always presented an ideal that has motivated various forms of experiments with communal life in the history of Christianity. Might it function as such an ideal for us today? Why or why not?

I want to call this passage a fellowship of the Spirit while others might want to call it communism, using Marx's term. What are the similarities and differences between Luke and Marx?

Is the mutual sharing and distribution of goods to all who have need a viable way of life today? Why or why not?

CHAPTER 7

Describe the spiritual and political aspects of the Spirit-anointed ministry of Jesus.

How did the Old Testament Jubilee year and the "year of the Lord's favor" that Jesus proclaimed come to be represented in the early Christian community? Why are these concepts so difficult for our contemporary ears?

What does it mean to say that the Spirit who worked through Jesus also has been poured out upon and given to his followers?

CHAPTER 8

How does Luke's story of the man healed at the temple gate (Acts 3) continue his theme of the restoration of Israel? What role do the Old Testament Scriptures play here and elsewhere in the unfolding of this Lukan thesis?

Why were the temple leaders interested in preserving the status quo? How did the healing of this man at the temple gate threaten their interests?

What are the economic and political implications of the Lukan message of healing for charismatic Christianity in our time?

CHAPTER 9

Why or how are we conditioned to emphasize the medical aspects of these miraculous healings of Jesus and not their public dimensions? How legitimate are the latter as presented in this chapter?

First-century Palestinian society was structured according to patron-client relations, such as that between centurion patrons and the people (their clients) they protected. How did Jesus' ministry overturn or at least threaten to dismantle such hierarchical structures?

Are modern-day healings in Christian circles signs of the coming kingdom of God? If this is the case, how might these signs change our perspective on and even our practices regarding the ministry of healing?

CHAPTER 10

Here we see a second representation of the fellowship of the Spirit (Acts 4:32–35); compare and contrast it with the first account (Acts 2:42–47).

Compare and contrast also Barnabas with Ananias and Sapphira. Is the punishment of the latter unduly harsh in light of the thesis being argued in this chapter and in this book?

Isn't Barnabas just an unusually generous figure, and isn't he just incidental to Luke's story (only two verses are devoted to him)? Or is Luke trying to make a normative theological and ethical point? Why would we rather believe the former about Barnabas rather than the latter?

CHAPTER 11

There is a lot of talk about Jesus hanging out with tax collectors, prostitutes, and other social outcasts. Who would be the equivalent of such in our world?

Are we more likely to empathize with Simon the Pharisee or the sinner woman? The synagogue leaders or the bent over and crippled woman? Why and what are the implications of our proclivities?

Is it really possible in today's world for Spirit-led disciples of Jesus to practice his vision of a world without hierarchies or social classes?

CHAPTER 12

Most of us who have time to do Bible studies such as this one are not being persecuted for our faith. Can we stand in solidarity and prayer with our brothers and sisters around the world who are currently experiencing the kind of persecution that this chapter's readings tell us happened to the disciples?

Talk about Herod as a representative of lord and savior Caesar, and how Luke's narrative reflects what it means to understand the lordship and salvation of Christ.

How do we understand the disciples' nonviolent resistance in our time? What are the political implications of such a stance for vital Christian discipleship?

CHAPTER 13

Isn't Jesus' passion unique to him? Can we really follow in the footsteps of Christ in his suffering?

To what degree is early Christian nonviolence an imitation of the founder of the Way?

Why is forgiveness central to a charismatic ethic of non-violence or a way of peacemaking? How is such forgiveness possible in the real world?

CHAPTER 14

How might experiences of immigrants in the United States especially since 1965 illuminate what happened in Acts 6 between Greek-speaking and Hebrew-speaking congregations?

Why is it important in addressing any leadership vacuum that charismatic leaders be appointed who represent the interests of the people they are leading? What are the implications of this principle in our contemporary multicultural, multiethnic, and globalized world?

Antioch was originally a "mission field" for missionaries from Jerusalem, but the Antiochene church came to the rescue of their mother church in the latter's time of need; are we in the Anglo-American West ready to receive the ministerial assistance of churches in the global South that we formerly considered to be our mission fields? What are the implications of this "reverse" missionary enterprise?

CHAPTER 15

Why are Jesus' teachings on wealth and poverty too uncomfortable for many of us?

Consider the story of the rich man and Lazarus: Is the only point of this story that those of us who are more well off should share with those more needy?

What about the Jubilee principle in the background of Luke's vision of the renewal of Israel? Are there any structural economic dimensions to the restoration of Israel and the coming kingdom?

CHAPTER 16

Stephen tells the story of ancient Israel from a Hellenistic Jewish perspective; what are the political implications of such an account (think about how the story of America might be told from the perspective of an American expatriate)?

Why were other Hellenistic Jews—"freedmen," Luke calls them (Acts 6:9)—so opposed to Stephen's message (think about how refugees from a country under occupation might have a vested interest in the restoration of their country)? How did this incident involving Stephen set up the tensions that we will see in the rest of the book of Acts?

Why are Stephen's theology, ministry, and life so important for the Spirit-empowered expansion of the gospel to the Gentiles? Can we appreciate his sacrifice today, two thousand years after his martyrdom?

CHAPTER 17

How did Stephen understand the role of the temple, and how might this understanding have been threatening to the temple leaders?

What was Jesus' attitude toward Jerusalem, and what are the implications of his "theology of Jerusalem" for us today?

The author of *Who Is the Holy Spirit?* follows scholars such as N. T. Wright in seeing the legacy of Jesus' ministry as related to redirecting Jewish nationalism: the emphasis on a way of peace averts destruction, whereas overzealous nationalism culminates in the wrath of Rome—witness the destruction that unfolded within a generation after Jesus' death. Talk about the implications of this message for understanding Luke's account (believed by most to have been written not too long after the destruction of Jerusalem in 70 CE) and what that means for us today.

CHAPTER 18

How did the expansion of the gospel into Samaria and the reception of the gospel by the Samaritans upset the Jewish worldview of the earliest followers of Jesus?

Review the entire passage devoted to the Good Samaritan (Luke 10:25–37): what are the implications of this narrative for people who we do not consider to be legitimate Christians?

Is it legitimate to view the Samaritans as "religious others" to Jews? What are the implications of our response to this question for a Spirit-inspired understanding of and interaction with people in non-Christian faiths today?

CHAPTER 19

Why is it legitimate from a biblical perspective to classify the eunuch under the "disability" category, and what are the implications of this classification?

Like the eunuch, Zacchaeus the dwarf is also accepted as Jesus' disciple just as he is, without any miraculous healing or fix. Are you comfortable with people with disabilities representing the gospel?

There are people with disabilities present at the eschatological banquet in Jesus' teaching (Luke 14:15–24). What are the implications of such images for our theology of disability? Our theology of salvation? Our theology of the afterlife?

CHAPTER 20

Was St. Paul impaired in any way? How might we understand his life, charismatic ministry, and Spirit-centered theology differently if he were?

Like Stephen, Paul was also a Hellenistically informed Jew. Why was this important for the one whom God raised up to be the apostle to the Gentiles?

With the introduction to Paul's ministry, the idea that the restoration of Israel included the Gentiles comes into focus. Why was this such a foreign notion to first-century Jews?

CHAPTER 21

We have often understood conversion in spiritual and individual terms. But what are the public or political aspects of conversion in the Gospel accounts discussed in this chapter?

One of the most challenging aspects of conversion is re-placement in (or, "among the members of") the family of God. What are the implications of this for biological family relations?

Isn't conversion about securing a place in heaven in the afterlife? Why does Jesus talk instead about orienting our Spirit-filled perspectives to the coming kingdom of God?

CHAPTER 22

We have long marveled at the biological miracle involved in the raising from the dead of the son of the widow of Nain. Now, what are the public aspects of this resuscitation that we have overlooked?

How was Tabitha's resurrection also the revitalization of an entire community?

We see in this chapter that resurrection accounts are also, like healings, signs of the kingdom. What are the implications of these accounts for contemporary Spirit-filled life and ministry?

CHAPTER 23

What does Luke seem to be more interested in: telling of Cornelius' salvation or telling of Peter's realization of the inclusion of the Gentiles in the redemptive plan of God? What textual clues can you provide for your response?

God "shows no partiality" (Acts 10:34): what are the implications of this statement for the thesis of this book about the Spirit's work in the wider world?

Can we speak of Cornelius as being instrumental in the conversion of Peter? Why or why not?

CHAPTER 24

If the restoration of Israel was divinely intended all along to include the Gentiles, then do we have sufficient indication of this in Luke's Gospel story of Jesus' life, ministry, and teachings?

Why is Jesus' proclamation of peace so important for a book on the political dimensions of Spirit-led discipleship?

In our lives and ministry today, to say that the gospel is for the Gentiles does not seem to pack much punch, probably because most if not all of us are Gentiles. How might we now need to translate this central thrust of the gospel in order for it to meaningfully engage our world, our time, and our situation?

CHAPTER 25

How does the story of Bar-Jesus illuminate the political dimensions of the spiritual world? Some would say that there is a danger in spiritualizing the political domain of demonizing our political opponents; if this is so, how should we then proceed?

Are exorcisms also signs of the coming kingdom? Do you believe that there are other physical signs of the impending reign of God?

Some say that one of the major reasons why the gospel has spread quickly across the global South is that most indigenous religious and cultural traditions have cosmologies and worldviews that are very similar to those of the New Testament (for example, involving evil spirits in relationship to healing). Can you see dangers to overemphasizing this point? Why might it be important to emphasize the public aspects of deliverance ministries instead?

CHAPTER 26

What are the public aspects of Jesus' encounter with and temptations by Satan in the wilderness?

A number of biblical scholars have suggested that the Gerasene demoniac had internalized the oppressive rule of imperial Rome. Discuss the merits of this thesis.

What are the political implications, if any, of the displacement of the kingdom of the devil with the reign of God in the Spirit-filled life and ministry of Jesus?

CHAPTER 27

The Jews were told that they "will be saved through the grace of the Lord Jesus, just as they [the Gentiles] will" (Acts 15:11). This might be analogous to Christians being told that they "will be saved through the grace of the Lord Jesus, just as they [put in any other group that is considered to be oppressive of Christians here] will." How ludicrous, or not, is this parallel?

The Jewish followers of Jesus wanted the Gentiles to become just like Jews (that is, to be circumcised) in order to "be saved." What are our assumptions and expectations today for non-Christians to be saved?

What is the danger of overemphasizing the universality of the Spirit's work? How might emphasizing also the particularity of the Spirit's work help to resolve this tension, and what does that mean for Christian mission today?

CHAPTER 28

We have often spiritualized and internalized the story of the Prodigal Son. What are the advantages of reading this story in terms of the renewal of Israel as including the Gentiles?

Are there many or few who will be saved? What are the implications of our answers to this question?

What happened to the Jews who did not embrace God's program of renewing Israel and redeeming the world? What might happen to us today if we don't accept and receive God's Spirit-empowered program of redemption?

CHAPTER 29

Among the Gospel writers, the role of women is most prominent in Luke's writings. What are the implications of what he says in Acts for our views regarding women in ministry today? What else might remain to be done on this matter?

Does the Holy Spirit still speak through visions and dreams today? Why or why not? What are the challenges and possibilities inherent in our response?

Timothy was of mixed ethnicity (a Jewish mother and a Greek father). How might his life provide insights into our own widespread experiences of hybridity and interraciality today?

CHAPTER 30

Are you comfortable with identifying Jesus as a "protofeminist"? Why or why not? Be sure to interact with the Lukan witness in detail in your response.

What does it mean to follow the Spirit-inspired Christ with regard to our attitudes regarding and actions toward women in a male-dominated world?

Is there a difference between the ministry of women and their role or roles in nonministerial contexts such as the home? How might we respond to this question in light of Luke and Acts?

CHAPTER 31

How does the story of the Pythonness break all kinds of stereotypical Christian beliefs about divination?

Flesh out what the author calls the "politics of prayer and praise" as exemplified in the Philippian jail. What are the implications for political engagement today for a Spirit-renewed Christianity?

What are the "politics of citizenship" in light of the Apostle Paul's experiences at Philippi?

CHAPTER 32

How would it feel to utter the Lord's Prayer (as Luke records it) as a mode of political engagement? Discuss each line in this regard.

Luke's version of the Lord's Prayer concludes with the promise that God will honor all authentic prayer by giving of his Spirit; think further now about the public and political dimensions of the outpouring of the Spirit on all flesh.

We often think about justice and justification in individual terms; how does the parable of the widow and the judge expand these horizons? Is this a legitimate expansion of the traditional doctrine of justification?

CHAPTER 33

At the Areopagus, Paul cited pagan poets and philosophers. What are the implications of this for our own engagement with culture and philosophical traditions?

A few decades ago, H. Richard Neibuhr presented a fivefold paradigm of Christ in relationship to culture:

- Christ against Culture. History is the story of a rising church or Christian culture and a dying pagan civilization.
- Christ of Culture. History is the story of the Spirit's encounter with nature and human culture.
- Christ above Culture. History is a period of preparation under law, reason, gospel, and church for an ultimate communion of the soul with God.
- Christ and Culture in Paradox. History is the time of struggle between faith and unbelief, a period between the giving of the promise of life and its fulfillment.
- Christ Transforming Culture. History is the story of God's mighty deeds and humanity's response to them. Christians taking this view live somewhat less "between the times" and somewhat more in the divine "now" than do the followers listed above. They are more concerned with the divine possibility of a present renewal than with conserving what has been given in creation or preparing for what will be given in a final redemption.

Discuss these views in light of our chapter.

Does the Spirit's redemptive work include the cultural, philosophical, and even religious traditions of the world? Why or why not? If you answer yes in any way, how?

CHAPTER 34

"Love your enemies." Is this easy? Is it easier at an interpersonal level or at a political level? Is it possible politically?

"Forgive us our debts even as we forgive the debts of others." Is this easy? Is it easier at an interpersonal level or at a political level? Is it possible politically?

We have traditionally thought about the Lukan metaphor of "turning the world upside down" (Acts 17:6) in terms of its Christianization; what if we now thought about this in terms of the work of the Spirit in the domains of social values, economic arrangements, and political structures? Is this a valid extrapolation of this metaphor?

CHAPTER 35

What can we learn from the encounter between Christianity and the religion of Artemis for interfaith relations in our time?

How did the economics of Ephesus have religious implications? What are the economic implications for Spirit-empowered mission today?

How are economics and religion bound up in our world? In Christianity? Is this good, bad, or unavoidable?

CHAPTER 36

For Paul, what was the connection between the resurrection of Jesus and the restoration of Israel?

Are there any public or political connections for our present belief in the Resurrection as the work of the Spirit? Should there be?

Paul was willing to be martyred for his belief in the resurrection of Jesus (and the restoration of Israel); what are we willing to be martyred for today? Should we be willing to be martyred for anything?

CHAPTER 37

Is it appropriate to think that there are cosmic dimensions to the Spirit's outpouring as suggested in this chapter? Why or why not?

Is "salvation" as plain as physical safety as suggested by the various uses of the Greek word *soteria* in Acts 27? What are the implications of this for mission, if any?

Jesus' rebuking the winds and waves (Luke 8:24) suggests he is operating under a similar authority as when he rebukes evil spirits. What are the pros and cons of viewing natural forces as parallel to principalities and powers?

CHAPTER 38

How was table fellowship also a sociopolitical and economic undertaking in first-century Palestinian culture? What can we learn about the theological commitments and vision of the followers of the Jesus movement from their eating habits?

Why and how might our practice of the Lord's Supper or the Eucharist also have public or political ramifications today?

What are the missional implications of mealtimes in today's world? Describe the contours of a Spirit-led and Spirit-filled way of eating in a pluralistic world.

CHAPTER 39

How do Paul's interactions with the Maltese "barbarians" challenge our missionary paradigm today?

How could we be better hosts in the public square of our multiethnic, multicultural, and multireligious world? And how can we be better guests in these same environments?

What does it mean for us to add to the twenty-ninth chapter of the book of Acts and to continue the story of the Spirit being poured out on all flesh?

Acknowledgments

*T*HIS BOOK was originally conceived in response to a request by Lil Copan, formerly one of the acquisitions editors at Paraclete Press, who had read Roger Olson's summary of my work in *Christianity Today* titled: "A Wind That Swirls Everywhere: Pentecostal Scholar Amos Yong Thinks He Sees the Holy Spirit Working in Other Religions, Too" (in March 2006). Lil contacted me to contribute to a series of books on the Spirit and spirituality for Paraclete Press. About a year later, I floated the idea of such a topic focused on the Holy Spirit to Anita Killebrew, the executive associate pastor at Great Bridge Presbyterian Church in Chesapeake, Virginia, where our family had been attending, for one of the church's adult Sunday school class offerings. It was received with enthusiasm, and a group of about fifteen of us (give or take a half dozen on any given Sunday), read Luke and Acts and discussed them for most of the 2008 calendar year.

Many thanks to Anita, who provided enough funds from the church's Christian education fund to purchase a number of commentaries for this project (some of which are listed in the bibliography). Thanks also to the following members of the Cornerstone class, some of whom were present for large segments of the discussion, a few of whom were faithful for almost each week of the entire eleven-month study, but all of whom contributed in some way to this book via the questions they asked or the comments they shared during our time together: Hank Bedell, Laura and Mike Boron, Carolyn and Bob Creekmore, Veronica DeSmit, Beth

Doriani, Jim Downey, Sara Green, Sonya Hall, Joyce and Mike Holden, Rob Holroyd, John Lynch, Shar Yeo and Timothy Lim Teck Ngern, Eliza and Andrew Marks, Melody and Chris Mendoza, Marian and John Neefus, Brooke Nielson, Wayne Pittman, Trudi and Doug Rauch, Sandy Sayre, Judy and Bob Steinmetz, Gail Trzcinski, and Alma Yong.

I also had students in my "Renewal and Politics" seminar during the summer 2009 semester at Regent University School of Divinity read and interact with the manuscript version of this book. I appreciate especially the following students for their perceptive observations that have improved the book: Mary Fast, Timothy Lim Teck Ngern, Hunter Hanger, Nicholas Daniels, and Theresa Demby.

I am grateful also to the following friends and colleagues, each of whom are specialists in the guild of New Testament studies in general and in Luke-Acts in particular, for their comments on an earlier draft of this manuscript: Michelle Lee-Barnewall, Thomas E. Phillips, James B. Shelton, and Martin W. Mittelstadt. As this is my first attempt to write in the area of biblical interpretation, their feedback has been very helpful in keeping me from making otherwise egregious errors as I venture outside my field of training (theology and religious studies) and attempt a responsible interpretation of these Lukan texts.

Needless to say, none of the aforementioned persons should be held responsible for the views expressed in this book, and whatever infelicities that remain are a result of my own stubbornness.

Thanks again to Lil Copan at Paraclete for helping me conceive the book and clarify its overall scope and approach. I also received a great deal of help from the Press's editors, especially Jon Sweeney and Jeff Reimer. Each has been invaluable in teaching me to write better for a nonacademic audience. Last but not least, Sr. Mercy Minor, Sr. Madeleine Cleverly, Karen Minster, and others at the Press have worked diligently in the production and publicity phases of this project, and I am grateful for their professionalism.

As always, Patty Hughson and her interlibrary loan staff here at Regent University have been indispensable in helping me secure the books and articles I've needed for this study, a far longer list than the one that appears in the select bibliography that follows.

Words also cannot express the debt I owe to my wife, Alma, for what she does from day to day that frees me up to read and write. In this case, she was also a faithful member of the Sunday school class and patiently endured the many weekend (especially Sunday afternoon) hours—my "spare time" devoted to church-related commitments—during the calendar year 2008, when I drafted the first version of the book manuscript. A more wonderful wife no man has and I am certainly undeserving.

Last, this book is dedicated to Alyssa, my oldest daughter, who by the time the book comes off the press will be ending her freshman year in college, one year earlier than expected. My little girl is transitioning away from home, but the world that will soon receive her also belongs to the Holy Spirit—so I send her off to make a difference in this world with prayers, committing her to the grace and power of the Spirit, and with all my love!

Notes

1   Having said this, I should also say that our bringing contemporary questions to the text does not mean we will be ignoring the texts' own concerns or the author's intentions. To be sure, there are a host of unresolved issues about who the author was (tradition says Luke, but even if that were right, we may not know much else about him). Scholars continue to dispute where and when it was written. (I favor Asia Minor, sometime during the last three decades of the first century CE, although there are a few scholars who posit Rome or Caesarea as well as think either that the abrupt ending of Acts suggests it was completed sometime before the fall of Jerusalem in 70 CE or that it draws from early second-century material that therefore places it during this later time.) The audience of Luke and Acts remains obscure. (Yes, they were addressed to Theophilus—according to Lk. 1:3 and Acts 1:1—but was Theophilus a Roman God-fearer, proselyte to Judaism, or follower of Jesus, and what about the wider community of which Theophilus may have been a part?) And the major questions regarding why these volumes were written continues to elicit discussion. While a definitive response to these questions will for the most part not impinge on the interpretations that follow, in some cases there will be implications, and we will at those moments provide further rationale for the very cursory responses above.

2   Thus does the Hebrew Bible frequently connects the restoration of Israel with the forgiveness of sins—e.g., Isa. 40:1–2; 43:25–44:3; Lam. 4:22; Jer. 31:31–34; 33:4–11; Ezek. 36:24–33.

3   The following summarizes what is described as the Year of Jubilee in Lev. 25:8–12 and Deut. 15:1–7.

4   The Greek word *ekklēsia* usually referred to the "assembly" of the Greek *polis* or city state; here and in the few other places it appears in Acts, it indicates the newly formed political community of messianic believers.

5   The "innocent victims" of Herod's politics, however, might have been the soldiers (and their families) who lost their lives because they had lost their prisoner, Peter (12:19).

6   It may be that Luke had other apologetic purposes in mind since late-night meetings in the first century were often surreptitious and clandestine, were thought to be related to politically suspicious activities, or involve sexually immoral or other grossly despicable behaviors such as human sacrificial rituals. Luke's noting that "there were many lamps in the room upstairs where we were meeting" (20:8), alongside his reporting of Eutychus's resuscitation, may have been intended to counter such suspicions regarding the early Jesus movement.

7   While the textual evidence is here almost equally divided (with the Septuagint saying seventy and the Masoretic Text saying seventy-two), there are at least two reasons for reading Luke as intending the latter. First, there are seventy-two generations of Jesus' genealogy (3:23–38), which goes all the way back to Adam and thus signifies the universality of Jesus' pedigree. Second, given Luke's understanding of the scope of the gospel as extending to the ends of the earth, his referencing of the nations present on the Day of Pentecost (Acts 2:7–11) may well have been a representative sample of the seventy-two nations in the Jewish "Table of Nations" tradition (Gen. 1 and 1 Chron. 1).

8   Luke includes references in the Gospel to Elizabeth, Mary's cousin (1:5), Anna the prophetess (2:36), Simon's mother-in-law (4:38), the widow of Nain (7:11), a sinful woman (7:37), the hemorrhaging woman (8:43), and the crippled woman (13:11), among others.

9   There are at least six Marys in the New Testament: the mother of Jesus; Mary Magdalene; the mother of James and John (24:1); the wife of Clopas (John 19:25); the mother of John Mark (Acts

12:12); and the sister of Martha and Lazarus, whom we are now discussing.

10 Paul may have taken a Nazirite vow that extended for a period of time, during which he did not cut his hair (Num. 6:1–21). We do know that Paul kept the law (e.g., Acts 21:18–26), including the rite of circumcision, which was performed on Timothy (16:3).

11 So not only does Paul repeatedly link his persecution to his beliefs about the resurrection of Jesus (Acts 24:14–15, 21; 25:19; 26:6–8, 23; 28:20), but he also insists in response that this hope was intertwined with the fate, future, and restoration of Israel and the Gentiles (22:15, 21; 26:17–20, 23; cf. 9:15; 13:47; 18:6).

12 Acts 21–26 covers Paul's arrival at Jerusalem, his subsequent captivity there and at Caesarea, and his self-defenses in these locales—all of which occurred over a period of two to three years.

13 But there is no justification for thinking of Luke as being anti-Semitic in his concluding Acts in this way. Rather, according to the mysterious providential workings of God, it was precisely the persecution of the Jewish followers of the Messiah that led originally to the gospel's going beyond the confines of Jerusalem and Judea into Samaria and the wider Diaspora, and it had been the ongoing rejection in the synagogues that also drove Paul to proclaim the gospel on the streets of Philippi, on Mars Hill, and in Tyrannus's lecture hall, among other places. Paul himself understood all of this as having been orchestrated by God "until the full number of the Gentiles has come in. And so all Israel will be saved" (Rom. 11:25–26).

Select Bibliography

I consulted many excellent commentaries for this book. The most important and helpful to me were the following:

Bock, Darrell L. *Acts*. Baker Exegetical Commentary on the New Testament. Grand Rapids: Baker Academic, 2007.

Dunn, James D. G. *The Acts of the Apostles*. Epworth Commentaries. London: Epworth, 1996.

Gaventa, Beverly Roberts. *The Acts of the Apostles*. Abingdon New Testament Commentaries. Nashville: Abingdon, 2003.

Green, Joel B. *The Gospel of Luke*. New International Commentary on the New Testament. Grand Rapids: Eerdmans, 1997.

Johnson, Luke Timothy. *The Acts of the Apostles*. Sacra Pagina 5. Collegeville, MN: Liturgical, 1992.

———, *The Gospel of Luke*. Sacra Pagina 3. Collegeville, MN: Liturgical, 1991.

Malina, Bruce J., and John J. Pilch. *Social-Science Commentary on the Book of Acts*. Minneapolis: Fortress, 2008.

Spencer, F. Scott. *Journeying through Acts: A Literary-Cultural Reading*. Peabody, MA: Hendrickson, 2004.

Talbert, Charles H. *Reading Luke: A Literary and Theological Commentary on the Third Gospel*. Rev. ed. Macon, GA: Smyth & Helwys, 2002.

Witherington, Ben III. *The Acts of the Apostles: A Socio-Rhetorical Commentary*. Grand Rapids: Eerdmans, 1998.

The following are only a few of the more accessible studies among the many that I consulted for this book:

Arlandson, James Malcolm. *Women, Class and Society in Early Christianity: Models from Luke-Acts*. Peabody, MA: Hendrickson, 1997.

Borg, Marcus J. *Conflict, Holiness and Politics in the Teachings of Jesus*. Studies in the Bible and Early Christianity 5. Lewiston, NY: Edwin Mellen, 1984.

Carter, Warren. *The Roman Empire and the New Testament: An Essential Guide.* Nashville: Abingdon, 2006.

Cassidy, Richard J. *Jesus, Politics, and Society: A Study of Luke's Gospel.* Maryknoll, NY: Orbis, 1978.

Conzelmann, Hans. *The Theology of St. Luke.* Translated by Geoffrey Buswell. 1961; reprint, Philadelphia: Fortress, 1982.

Crossan, John Dominic. *God and Empire: Jesus against Rome, Then and Now.* San Francisco: HarperSanFrancisco, 2007.

Gillman, John. *Possessions and the Life of Faith: A Reading of Luke-Acts.* Collegeville, MN: Liturgical, 1991.

Green, Joel B. *The Theology of the Gospel of Luke.* Cambridge: Cambridge University Press, 1995.

Hanson, K. C., and Douglas E. Oakman. *Palestine in the Time of Jesus: Social Structures and Social Conflicts.* Minneapolis: Fortress, 1998.

Horsley, Richard A. *Jesus and Empire: The Kingdom of God and the New World Disorder.* Minneapolis: Fortress, 2003.

Jervell, Jacob. *The Theology of the Acts of the Apostles.* Cambridge: Cambridge University Press, 1996.

Johnson, Luke Timothy. *Sharing Possessions: Mandate and Symbol of Faith.* Minneapolis: Fortress, 1981.

Levine, Amy-Jill, with Marianne Blickenstaff, eds. *A Feminist Companion to Luke.* London: Sheffield Academic Press, 2003.

———, eds. *A Feminist Companion to the Acts of the Apostles.* London: Sheffield Academic Press, 2004.

Levinskaya, Irina. *The Book of Acts in Its First Century Setting,* vol. 5, *The Book of Acts in Its Diaspora Setting.* Grand Rapids: Eerdmans, 1996.

Moxnes, Halvor. *The Economy of the Kingdom: Social Conflict and Economic Relations in Luke's Gospel.* Philadelphia: Fortress, 1988.

Neyrey, Jerome H., ed. *The Social World of Luke-Acts: Models for Interpretation.* Peabody, MA: Hendrickson, 1991.

Oakman, Douglas E. *Jesus and the Peasants.* Eugene, OR: Cascade, 2008.

Parsons, Mikeal C. *Body and Character in Luke and Acts: The Subversion of Physiognomy in Early Christianity.* Waco: Baylor University Press, 2006.

Phillips, Thomas E. *Reading Issues of Wealth and Poverty in Luke-Acts*. Studies in the Bible and Early Christianity 48. Lewiston, NY: Edwin Mellen, 2001.

Rapske, Brian. *The Book of Acts and Paul in Roman Custody*. Grand Rapids: Eerdmans, 1994.

Ravens, David. *Luke and the Restoration of Israel*. Journal for the Study of the New Testament Supplement Series 119. Sheffield: Sheffield Academic Press, 1995.

Samkutty, V. J. *The Samaritan Mission in Acts*. Library of New Testament Studies 328. London: T & T Clark, 2006.

Schmidt, Thomas E. *Hostility to Wealth in the Synoptic Gospels*. Journal for the Study of the New Testament Supplement Series 15. Sheffield: JSOT Press, 1987.

Shelton, James B. *Mighty in Word and Deed: The Role of the Holy Spirit in Luke-Acts*. Peabody, MA: Hendrickson, 1991.

Stronstad, Roger. *The Prophethood of All Believers: A Study in Luke's Charismatic Theology*. Journal of Pentecostal Theology Supplement Series 16. Sheffield: Sheffield Academic Press, 1999.

Turner, Max. *Power from on High: The Spirit in Israel's Restoration and Witness in Luke-Acts*. Journal of Pentecostal Theology Supplement Series 9. Sheffield: Sheffield Academic Press, 1996.

Walaskay, Paul W. *"And So We Came to Rome": The Political Perspective of St. Luke*. Cambridge: Cambridge University Press, 1983.

Wall, Robert W., and Anthony B. Robinson. *Called to Be Church: The Book of Acts for a New Day*. Grand Rapids: Eerdmans, 2006.

Wenk, Matthias. *Community-Forming Power: The Socio-Ethical Role of the Spirit in Luke-Acts*. Journal of Pentecostal Theology Supplemental Series 19. Sheffield: Sheffield Academic Press, 2000.

Wright, Tom. *The Original Jesus: The Life and Vision of a Revolutionary*. Grand Rapids: Eerdmans, 1996.

Yoder, John Howard. *The Politics of Jesus*. Grand Rapids: Eerdmans, 1972.

Index

⌐ Giver of Life ⌐

Contents

Giver of Life: The Holy Spirit in Orthodox Tradition
FR. JOHN W. OLIVER | ISBN 978-1-55725-675-1

HOW DOES ONE LIVE A LIFE GUIDED BY THE HOLY SPIRIT?

This series of PARACLETE GUIDES explores the richness of different Christian traditions and perspectives on the Holy Spirit.

Giver of Life
The Holy Spirit in Orthodox Tradition

Fr. John W. Oliver

*In Eastern Orthodoxy,
the Holy Spirit is where
the mystery of God comes alive!*

Delving deeply and subtly into Orthodox tradition and theology, *Giver of Life* articulates the East's perspective on the identity of the Holy Spirit as the third Person of the Trinity. Writing with the sensibility of a poet, John Oliver reflects on the relationship of the Holy Spirit to the Church, the world, and the human person.

"This life-giving book will instruct, inspire, and encourage all who are looking for life—in abundance."
— PROTOPRESBYTER THOMAS HOPKO, *dean emeritus, St. Vladimir's Orthodox Theological Seminary*

"Father Oliver introduces us not only to the Holy Spirit but to the Orthodox Church. As an evangelical, not surprisingly, I found things to disagree with. Then again, I also found myself writing on almost every page, 'Amen'!"
— MARK GALLI, author of *Beyond Smells and Bells: The Wonder and Power of Christian Liturgy*

FATHER JOHN W. OLIVER is the priest of St. Elizabeth Orthodox Christian Church in Murfreesboro, TN. A graduate of St. Tikhon's Orthodox Theological Seminary, he later joined their faculty as instructor in Old and New Testament and American Religious History. He lives in Tennessee with his wife, Lara, and their five children.

⤳ The Spirit Unfettered ⤳

Contents

The Spirit Unfettered: Protestant Views on the Holy Spirit
EDMUND J. RYBARCZYK, PH.D. | ISBN 978-1-55725-654-6

The Spirit Unfettered
Protestant Views on the Holy Spirit

Edmund J. Rybarczyk, Ph.D.

This clear guide will help you understand what is distinctive about Protestant perspectives on who the Holy Spirit is and what the Holy Spirit does in our lives.

The Spirit Unfettered takes you on a journey through five centuries of Christians trying to understand what it means to know God in the Holy Spirit. After an introduction that broadly compares Protestant perspectives with Roman Catholic and Eastern Orthodox models, the understandings of important theologians and pivotal figures are explored in detail.

"We can be grateful to God that so many Christians in recent years have experienced the power of the Holy Spirit in new ways. But the time is long past for the whole Church to claim that renewing power, both theologically and experientially. This fine book points us to the theological resources—drawn from a variety of Christian traditions—to move ahead with that urgent task!"

—Dr. Richard J. Mouw, president, Fuller Theological Seminary

The result is an even-handed, thorough, and illuminating story of how Christians have come to know and explain the work of the Holy Spirit since the Protestant Reformation.

Edmund J. Rybarczyk, Ph.D., is associate professor of historic and systematic theology at Vanguard University in Costa Mesa. His book, *Beyond Salvation: Eastern Orthodoxy and Classical Pentecostalism on Becoming Like Christ* won the Pneuma Book Award, given by the Society for Pentecostal Studies for the outstanding publication in Pentecostal scholarship each year. He was managing editor of *Pneuma: The Journal of the Society for Pentecostal Studies* for six years and is an ordained minister with the Assemblies of God. Rybarczyk lives with his wife, Tawnya, and three children in California.

ABOUT PARACLETE PRESS

Who We Are

Paraclete Press is a publisher of books, recordings, and DVDs on Christian spirituality. Our publishing represents a full expression of Christian belief and practice—from Catholic to Evangelical, from Protestant to Orthodox.

We are the publishing arm of the Community of Jesus, an ecumenical monastic community in the Benedictine tradition. As such, we are uniquely positioned in the marketplace without connection to a large corporation and with informal relationships to many branches and denominations of faith.

What We Are Doing

Books Paraclete publishes books that show the richness and depth of what it means to be Christian. Although Benedictine spirituality is at the heart of all that we do, we publish books that reflect the Christian experience across many cultures, time periods, and houses of worship. We publish books that nourish the vibrant life of the church and its people—books about spiritual practice, formation, history, ideas, and customs.

We have several different series, including the best-selling Paraclete Essentials and Paraclete Giants series of classic texts in contemporary English; A Voice from the Monastery—men and women monastics writing about living a spiritual life today; award-winning literary faith fiction and poetry; and the Active Prayer Series that brings creativity and liveliness to any life of prayer.

Recordings From Gregorian chant to contemporary American choral works, our music recordings celebrate sacred choral music through the centuries. Paraclete distributes the recordings of the internationally acclaimed choir Gloriæ Dei Cantores, praised for their "rapt and fathomless spiritual intensity" by *American Record Guide*, and the Gloriæ Dei Cantores Schola, which specializes in the study and performance of Gregorian chant. Paraclete is also the exclusive North American distributor of the recordings of the Monastic Choir of St. Peter's Abbey in Solesmes, France, long considered to be a leading authority on Gregorian chant.

DVDs Our DVDs offer spiritual help, healing, and biblical guidance for life issues: grief and loss, marriage, forgiveness, anger management, facing death, and spiritual formation.

Learn more about us at our website:
www.paracletepress.com, or call us toll-free at 1-800-451-5006.